A NEW CONSCIOUSNESS

THE TRUE SPIRIT OF NEW AGE

By Melody Baker

First Edition

New Thought Publishing
Duluth, GA

7/92

Library of Congress Catalog Card Number: 91-61598

Publisher's Cataloging in Publication
(Prepared by Quality Books Inc.)

Baker, Melody, 1952-
A new consciousness : the true spirit of New Age / by Melody Baker.
- 1st ed. -
p. cm.
Includes bibliographical references and index.
ISBN 0-9629449-1-2
1. New Age movement-United States. 2. New Age movement-United States-Personal narratives. 3. Spiritual life. I. Title.
BP605.N48   299.93   91-61598
              MARC

1 2 3 4 5 6 7 8 9   94 93 92 91

Printed in the United States of America

c.1

Contents

Acknowledgments

First and foremost, I want to thank the eight hundred and forty-nine people who took the time and effort to complete and return the surveys that formed the first phase of research for this book. Next, I want to express my gratitude and appreciation for the warmth and hospitality of the sixty people who welcomed me into their homes for personal interviews and shared the intimate details of their life and spiritual quest for the benefit of the readers of this book.

I must also thank my family and friends for their complete support since this project began three years ago. Thanks also to April, Ann, and Iris for their contributions in the editing process.

Finally, I thank God for the inspiration to write this book and for supplying me with the will to continue when things seemed overwhelming. I am also grateful for the opportunity that writing this book gave me to meet some wonderful people across the country, anyone of whom I would be pleased to call a friend.

"Most of us," said the cosmic humorist, "go through life not knowing what we want, but feeling darned sure *this isn't it*."

- Handbook to Higher Consciousness

1   Researching New Age

Do people outside New Age really know what New Age is all about? Based on media accounts and books by Christian authors, I think not. And how much do people pursuing New Age thought know about other people following a similar path? For many people, the answer is very little. My curiosity about New Age from the perspective of someone who was no longer fully outside yet not quite inside led to researching and writing this book.

In researching this book, I found that fear was a major culprit in this lack of knowledge. While many people are indifferent to or tolerant of spiritual paths other than their own, some people outside New Age fear that it represents some sort of threat to the safety and security of their religious beliefs. And when this fear is expressed in churches, on television, or in the workplace, some people pursuing New Age refrain from discussing an important part of their life for fear of ridicule or persecution. What neither group realizes is that for every New Ager visible to the public or their friends, there are many more who are invisibly working alone at discovering their personal realization of spiritual truth. And many of them are neighbors or co-workers.

For an indication as to the scope of New Age, let's look at a few magazine circulation figures included in *New Marketing Opportunities*, a guide to New Age marketing resources published by First Editions. It lists three national New Age/metaphysical magazines who claim circulations of over 100,000-*Body, Mind & Spirit* (150,000), *Fate Magazine* (128,000), and *New Age Journal* (180,000). And there are several regional New Age magazines in the United States and Canada listed with circulations of over 50,000 One New England magazine, *Earth Star Journal*, has a listed circulation of 180,000. Since it is doubtful that the same people are subscribers to all of these magazines, it is very likely that several hundred thousand people subscribe to New Age publications. Considering that many of the survey respondents weren't current subscribers to publications, the total number of people involved in New Age pursuits may easily fall into the millions.

You may have an idea now that New Agers are not isolated phenomena. And as you read this book, you will also see that they are similar to everyone else struggling with the meaning of life, except they don't have society's support. For many reasons, as you will read in the personal stories, they didn't find the support they needed in traditional religion for their spiritual search. But as they turn their beliefs into personal truth and inner knowing, they feel the confidence to reveal themselves to the world and are often surprised to find others they have known for years walking a similar path. If this book reduces the fear and misunderstanding of New Age in just one reader, it will have served its purpose.

To that end, I sought to answer questions I had about New Age as I began to explore that world, such as: Is New Age something to be afraid of? Why do people get involved, and how has it affected their lives? That inner aspect seemed to be missing from most accounts of New Age I had read, except for a few autobiographical books. And it seemed to me to be the most important measure of the potential influence of New Age. My interest grew into the desire to research and write a book about normal, everyday people involved in New Age, rather than the celebrities and the more well-known New Age personalities profiled in the media.

Most of the research for this book comes from a nationwide survey (see Appendix 1 for a copy of the survey) and individual interviews of subscribers to New Age publications. I created a survey to get answers to the questions mentioned above and more-background, reasons for involvement, growth techniques used, and the effect of New Age thought on ten major areas of their lives.

To satisfy both sides of the brain, I have included statistics for the analytical side and intimate personal stories of transformation for the sensitive side. For those who aren't in an analytical mode now, please bear with me while I supply numbers for those who are. Here goes.

I sent four thousand nine hundred and sixteen surveys to subscribers[1] of five regional New Age publications and one national New Age magazine from June 1988 to January 1989. I received eight hundred forty-nine replies, a response rate of seventeen and three-tenths percent. The

---

1. Subscribers were selected randomly from the following states-Alabama, Arizona, California, Colorado, Connecticut, Florida, Georgia, Hawaii, Illinois, Maine, Massachusetts, Minnesota, Nevada, New Hampshire, New Mexico, New York, North Carolina, South Carolina, Tennessee, Texas, Vermont, Virginia, and Washington.

statistical information from those surveys is included in several chapters and Appendices.

I also asked for volunteers to be considered for personal interviews and received six hundred thirteen "yes" answers. From those, I selected a cross section of sixty respondents from seven regional areas and traveled to those areas to interview them from August 1988 to April 1989. The chapters containing personal stories and New Age concerns and advice are the results of those interviews. Those stories of crisis, growth, and transformation will give you detailed insight into these people, their involvement in New Age, and how they incorporate New Age thought into their daily lives.

Whether you have personal knowledge of New Age thought, are skeptical about it, or just curious to know more, this book was written for you. If you are consciously on a spiritual path, whether it has been for years or days, you will find inspiration and a sense of community in the stories of others on their spiritual journeys.

If you feel that something is missing inside, that there should be more to your life, especially peace, joy, and love, you will find evidence of others who have been where you are and have begun to fill that emptiness. You will read about the steps those people took to gain control of their lives and their happiness. Then you can decide if you want to apply any of them to your own life.

To those who are curious, skeptical, or fearful about New Age thought, this book may present belief systems, experiences, and activities that are unknown or uncomfortable for you. To fully experience this book, I urge you to set aside any preconceived ideas or judgments about New Age. And be aware of the effect what you read has on how you feel and what you think. You will feel either attraction, indifference, or rejection towards each part that you read.

If something attracts you, you can decide if and how you want to explore it later. If you are indifferent about something, it probably is not an issue for you now. But look closely at the ideas that disturb you. Are they in conflict with a current belief you hold? Which one would you rather hold? Do the ideas touch a part of you that is hidden from your conscious awareness? When you finish the book, you can decide whether to take up your old ideas or adjust them based on what you have read.

Next, we will look at the difficulty in defining the term "New Age."

2   What is New Age?

If anyone tells you they have a black and white answer to this question, you're asking the wrong person. New Age is a term that came into popular use in United States in the early 1980's and refers to a large collection of thought and activities that promotes personal and spiritual growth or transformation. It also focuses on the concept of wholeness of beings, society, and the planet. That means looking at physical, mental, emotional, and spiritual aspects and recognizing their interaction rather than thinking of the body or the planet as made of parts that can be healed or replaced without regard to the rest of the whole. New Age started in Western society with the influx of eastern teachings and the human potential movement of the late 1960's and 1970's[1].

Just as the term "Christian" includes many belief systems and denominations, some with very differing ideas, New Age covers a wide range of belief systems, almost as many are there are people involved in it. That is because one of the core beliefs of New Age is that each person has the right to develop a spiritual belief system based on personal experience and individual realization of spiritual truths. Dogma is disdained.

Some people involved in New Age feel the term has lost its meaning because it has been applied as a term of derision by the media, which often focuses on unusual outward trappings of some New Agers. And others who may not share the spirit behind New Age have taken on the label because they recognize its commercial potential. This broad and inconsistent use of the term makes it very difficult for those on the outside to understand what New Age truly is.

1.For a detailed history of the birth of New Age, see the book, *New Age Almanac*, by J. Gordon Melton, published in 1991 by Visible Ink Press.

My first step in studying the term was to research external perspectives of New Age written in newspapers, magazines, and in books by Christian authors. The media have used it as a term of skepticism for people who employ crystals, psychics, and channels to help them direct their lives. From a surface view, this impression is understandable, and the unusual sells more copy. But the external trappings used by some New Agers blind reporters from the real story, which is the process of change that people undergo. Their ways of thinking, their attitudes toward themselves, others, and the planet are making major shifts, the paradigm shifts mentioned in Marilyn Ferguson's book, *The Aquarian Conspiracy*.

Some conservative Christians use the "New Age" label as a rallying cry to inspire fear and to direct anger towards people they believe are agents of the devil. Using a label is dangerous because it stereotypes and dehumanizes. If you can label something, you don't have to think about it or look too closely to see what it is. But does it really fit the label you have given it and your associations with that label? Is that person really a threat or only someone with beliefs different from your own? Since some people believe that their religious beliefs are the only right beliefs and that they have a duty to carry them to every non-believer, one can understand their criticism of people who explore other spiritual paths. It is consistent with their beliefs.

To get an inside perspective on what the term New Age means, I asked for a definition on the survey form. For those skeptical about New Age, the answers may surprise you in their spiritual and peaceful nature. Answers were selected to represent the varied perspectives and are listed on the next few pages, grouped by common themes.

Spiritual

- "It is an age of conscious awareness-when we realize our spiritual selves and realize that what happens to us does not come from God 'out there' but from God 'in here'-our awareness of this has moved up from an unconscious level to conscious awareness."
- "An emerging emphasis on the spiritual dimension of life: a rediscovery of eternal truths that have been suppressed by an overemphasis on the 'rational and reasonable."
- "An era in which consciousness is expanding beyond the material world of things and now includes for more and more people awareness of spiritual energy, laws, and patterns."

- "The allowance of the spiritual values in the midst of physical activity. The blending of all levels together-spiritual, mental, emotional, and physical."
- "It means a newer, greater, better life as a spiritual being with Jesus Christ as the center and foundation of our being. Spiritual development is a personal adventure into 'self.' People are able to teach you the words which the left-brain can understand, but wisdom is in the heart. It comes with experience."

Existence of God

- "Aligning all our God given innate gifts to be the best we can be. Connecting to the idea of self as source of creation. Taking great personal responsibility to enhance life for all on Earth."
- "Awareness that God (or the Source) is in all beings; you are a path and a channel to spiritual awakening-we are all at different levels of enlightenment, but we are where we need to be for our growth."
- "A time when all individuals living on earth are being encouraged to know consciously and act upon the universal truths of God. Heaven and Earth are seeking to become one."
- "An interest in the whole person-body, mind, and spirit. The belief that we are all part of the energy force we call 'God' and that we all create our world/reality for the purpose of growth and to see what can be done with love."
- "Being closer to God. Getting in tune with the planet Earth, taking a closer look at God's creations. Helping in any way we can to improve the environment."
- "That you truly can have a personal relationship with God and Jesus. And in doing so, you may tap hidden spiritual potential."
- "Viewing life as perfection personified. Seeing the Christ in everyone. Knowing God is all in all. Realizing I am not material, but spiritual, and forever is my gift from Him. It's life and life, not life and death."

Connection to Others

- "New Age is the remembrance of the brotherhood/sisterhood of humankind. An openness to the infinite wonder of life."
- "People realizing how important they are to themselves and others. To stress love and service to all people. How important it is to be the best that you can be."
- "I see it as an awakening era for mankind on this planet where we will develop to a very advanced degree in our intuitive/psychic abilities and there will be intimate communication and trust between all beings as we realize our true divine nature and connect with the whole universe."
- "The New Age is a re-awakening of interest and understanding of knowledge that we have had for centuries. The underlying theory is both scientific and spiritual-and that is that we as human beings have everything we need; we just need to learn how to use it. Everything in the universe is connected and guided by a divine force."
- "A universal connecting and flow of consciousness; the Age of Enlightenment: a rent in the veil of darkness, ignorance, bigotry and other forms of solidified consciousness."
- "Knowing there is a greater reality beyond the human and physical and knowing it is infinitely loving. Knowing this life source infuses all beings and connects us with one another."

Acceptance/Openness

- "The New Age is to me made up of a collective body of free thinking individuals who are effecting change with new beliefs. Its progress could be said to be based on a sense of order within oneself amid chaos. A sense of spiritual fulfillment in place of dogma and guilt and a belief that love is at the core of each human being instead of fear and suspicion."
- "True realization as to why we're here and how we create our own life. My only problem with New Age is the tendency that all groups have to differentiate themselves from others because they're on the 'right' path. I have recently felt that I want to avoid New Age groups/functions because of the tendency for people (or

me) to think they're (or I'm) right and everyone else is wrong. But I remind myself we are all people with our own path to follow and I am no more right or wrong than anyone else is. I allow/accept/love people as they are."

- "I think of it as people becoming more open and less afraid of coming to terms with themselves, taking charge of their lives. There's less of a taboo to talk about personal problems than in the past. I'm not sure if crystals, channeling, etc. has anything to do with it."

- "Means a new beginning-a rebirth! It means cleaning house-getting rid of old ways of thinking, saying, doing, feeling, and being and replacing these old and often destructive ways of being with new and better ways! It means keeping an open mind and heart and continuing to grow through education and spiritual exploration."

Expanded Consciousness

- "A period in the evolution of the planet when personal consciousness expansion is possible as never before. A time when the opportunity to grow personally and worldwide is accelerated and assisted by Spirit."

- "A multi-faceted consciousness, which is being experienced by a wide range of people from various disciplines. It embraces the exploration, discovery, experience, and transformation of the Human Being (God-Man-Being) through many models and paradigms for the purpose of integration and wholeness."

Personal Responsibility/Control

- "Taking back responsibility and accountability for personal choice, decisions, and life direction."

- "The New Age is a time for individuals to take responsibility for their own lives-spiritually, mentally, and physically. A time of cleansing our minds, hearts, bodies, and souls. A time for taking care of ourselves first, then our families, communities, countries, and world."

Other

- "The falling away of all pictures about what you thought you were, of relationships, of ideas about what true spirituality is. You are truly left with nothing the way you thought it was-but what 'is' is not describable."
- "Learning that goals are not the answer. One does not become anything; all life is endless becoming."
- "A foretold period in human evolution when all incarnate, sentient beings have become enlightened and live in a golden age of harmony, love, peace, compassionate understanding, and highly creative endeavor."

Skeptical

There were skeptical responses even among subscribers to New Age publications:

- "An amalgam of people who are learning to become responsible for their destinies, most of them ain't making it."
- "I find the term New Age rather cliche and with some negative characteristics as well."
- "I view 'The New Age Movement' as a massive, misguided ill-fated ego trip where growth rates far behind having a good story."
- "I don't believe in the term. I think that it is a product of the media age where people have to define themselves in some way. I don't think 'New Age' people are different from anyone else except that they take themselves too seriously."

Summary

As you can see, agreement on a specific definition of New Age would be hard to find even among people who live its varied philosophies every day.

In general, the definition seems to include a commitment to spiritual growth which people pursue in different manners, many considered non-traditional in Western culture. A personal, dynamic relationship with God or some Higher Power usually evolves as the person begins to know himself and his Higher Power. Dogma and the absence of questioning are seen as obstacles to growth.

The mistake an outsider makes is focusing on the unusual tools or trappings of growth and change-such as crystals, astrology, visualization, affirmation, meditation, herbs or Tarot-with which he is not familiar and may therefore distrust. Most religions have rituals and "tools" that are unique to each and often strange to outsiders. But they shouldn't be confused with the truths they were developed to support and honor. Those truths are the real essence of the religion. With that in mind, someone unfamiliar with New Age should direct his vision and opinion instead to the process and effects of change in the person using a "New Age" tool-his change in consciousness and attitude toward life. The effects on society are felt every day as that consciousness grows and spreads in individuals.

What are those effects? From the interviews, I found that people are exchanging competition for cooperation. Some forego career advancement to maintain balance in their lives or to be of service to others. Some people find that pursuing work and a life-style they enjoy often results in less need for material goods and that their material needs are easily met. Others spend extra money and effort in order to conserve and recycle resources. Many have more tolerance, acceptance, and compassion because of their view that all life is spiritually connected, leaving them feeling more peaceful and happy. They take responsibility for their decisions and the resulting consequences while sometimes struggling to reconcile their spiritual beliefs with their physical reality. Emotions are accepted and valued as signals for what is right or wrong in one's life. Self-love and love of creation are on-going goals.

Simply put, that which is truly New Age respects all life and the planet. It values honesty and integrity in relationships and is committed to self-healing, wholeness, and self-acceptance. You will get a better idea of the variety of tools and how they are used in the personal stories and the chapter on growth techniques.

Some people believe there is a New Age conspiracy or movement with an agenda of its own. While there are organizations under the New Age umbrella that have agendas of their own beyond personal growth and transformation, you will see in the personal stories that respect for individual will and rights is valued above forcing change in others. Most of the people I surveyed and interviewed did not even belong to a New Age group. Most are working alone on their individual growth using books and occasional seminars. They want to change the world from the inside out by changing themselves. Our tendency to label and judge large groups based on a few members is an unfortunate habit. By closing ourselves off to whole groups, we miss out on potentially rewarding relationships with members of that group who are really not much different from us.

For another perspective on what New Age is, see the chart on the following page, which was reprinted by permission of the author, Jack Clarke. (See Appendix 6 for information on obtaining frameable copies.)

What is New Age, anyway?

It's people taking conscious responsibility for their own lives, not blaming others for their problems.

It's people who deliberately decide to learn and grow.

It's people that don't have to be right, except for themselves.

It's people seeing problems as lessons, perhaps in a long series of lives and lessons.

It's people who believe we are what we think we are, and can change ourselves by changing our thinking.

It's people that feel they can change the world by changing themselves, not by trying to change others.

It's people who search for strength from the universe by going inside themselves.

It's people that recognize love doesn't have to have conditions attached.

It's people loving and knowing themselves in order to better know and love others.

It's people who see others as not better than nor less than, but rather different than, themselves, yet part of the same whole.

It's people that choose their own path rather than follow dogma.

It's people honoring your right to your own path, not theirs.

It's people who realize that now is all we have, since yesterday is just a thought and so is tomorrow.

It's people interested in owning themselves rather than things.

It's people who see joy in life rather than pain, having experienced enough pain already.

It's people curious about extra sensory perception and all it implies.

It's people in all walks of life, from business persons to flower essence healers, psychologists to UFO investigators.

New Age is not a new religion with a hierarchy of priests and rituals, seeking converts, though some new agers choose some ritual.

New Age is not often gloom and doomers, though many are concerned about ecology, the economy and other forces that affect our world.

New Age is not a movement based on guilt, anger, fear or hurt; it is a journey toward the love that is God.

New Age is not allegiance to one master; it is learning from many masters in the quest for the oneness of God.

New Age could not become a cult because of what is said above.

New Age is not just humans doing, it is humans being.

© 1988   Jack Clarke

3   Who are New Agers?

As I mentioned in the first chapter, when I was first exposed to New Age, I was curious about the people involved. I wanted to know if there were a particular profile of the person who became involved. This chapter looks at some of those measurable characteristics as computed from the survey forms.

We will see that New Agers dont come from one income, age, or educational group. We will also look at their religious backgrounds, occupations, and relationship status among other characteristics. Finally, well look at the major reasons why they turned to New Age thought. For those of you still not in an analytical mode, feel free to move on to chapter 4 and the personal stories.

Figure 1 shows that nearly three-quarters of those involved in New Age are women. This agrees with a survey published in the May/June 1989 issue of the national New Age magazine Body, Mind & Spirit which found that 73% of their readers who responded were women. You will find different reasons for this given within New Age. One is that women are more open to admitting there are parts of themselves they would like to change. Another is that they are more open to exploring their spiritual aspects. And some equate New Age with a time of increasing feminine energy[1] being sent to the planet to balance the masculine energy[2], which has been the major influence in the world for so long.

1.Considered nurturing, receptive, creative and spiritual.
2. Described as concerned with the material world, action-oriented but lacking spiritual grounding.

Figure 1-By Sex

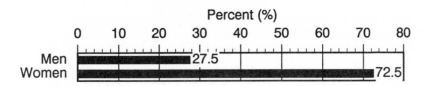

Figure 2 shows the breakdown by age and sex of those responding to the survey. For both groups, the ages of 30-50 contain the majority of respondents. The highest concentration for women is between the ages of 35 and 45 while for men it is from age 30 to 40. There are over twice the percent of people in New Age between the ages of 30 and 50 as there are in the general population (67% versus less than 30%).[3]

Figure 2-Age at Time of Survey

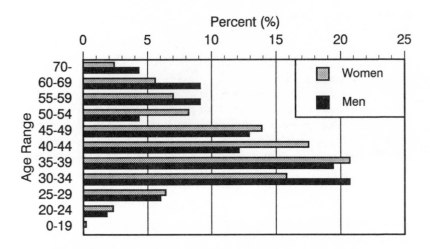

Only one person under age twenty responded. This may be because they are less likely to have personal subscriptions to the newspapers and magazine which provided names for the survey mailing. In addition, the personal stories reveal that most people were involved with a traditional

---

3. As documented in the 1989 *Statistical Abstract of the United States*, based on 1987 figures.

religion as a child and didnt become involved in New Age until they were on their own and decided their religion wasnt working for them.

Figure 3 shows the percent of men and women by the age ranges at which they seriously committed to their spiritual growth. (Question 34 on the survey.) The highest percentage age range for men (ages 20-24) starts five years earlier than the highest percentage range for women (ages 25-29).

Figure 3-Age at Commitment to Spiritual Growth

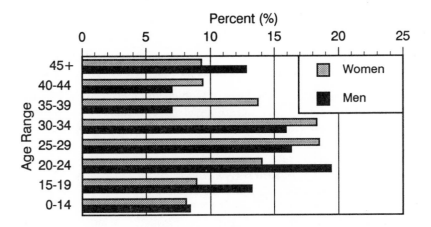

Figure 4 shows the percent of men and women by the number of years they have been committed to spiritual growth.[4] In both groups, over 50% have been serious about their growth for more than ten years.

Figure 4-By Number of Years of Growth

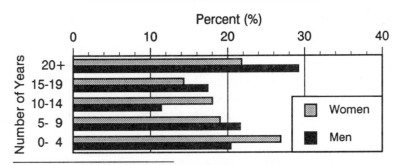

4. Calculated by subtracting age at commitment to spiritual growth (question 34 on the survey) from their age at the time of the survey.

Figure 5 shows a breakdown of respondents by race, showing that participation is skewed heavily to the white race. One reason may be the differences in spiritual cultures and traditions among the races.

Figure 5-By Race

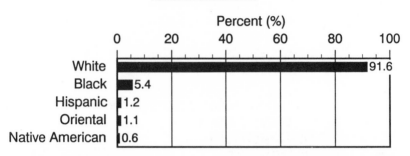

Figure 6 shows the breakdown of women and men according to the order of birth. There is a significantly smaller proportion of only children compared to those with siblings. That may be due to the proportion of only children in the general population.

Figure 6-By Order of Birth

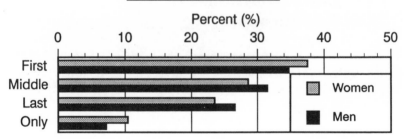

Figure 7 shows the religious background of the respondents. As a group, it would seem that a higher percentage of them (87%) have a formal religious background than the general population. According to *The World Almanac and Book of Facts 1990,* the highest percentage of the U.S. population claiming church membership in the last thirty years was 64% in 1960. This is quite a contrast with one Christian author s assertion that people who choose New Age arent familiar with traditional religion.

Many of the people interviewed credited their early religious training for sparking their interest in continuing their spiritual growth. The Body, Mind & Spirit survey mentioned earlier showed similar statistics for its readers-52% Protestant (51% in this survey), 27% Catholic, 3% Jewish, and 11% with no religious background. As you will see in the personal stories, although most of those interviewed have a traditional religious background, their religion did not meet their needs, so they looked for another path to answer their questions.

Figure 7-By Religious Background

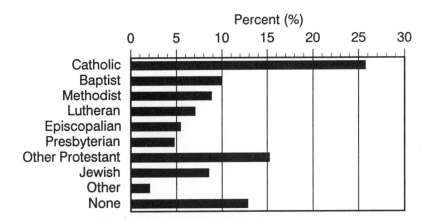

Figure 8 shows the percentage of respondents by highest education completed. Sixty-nine percent of the respondents have completed at least a two year college degree as compared with twenty percent of white adults in the general population.[5] Only four-tenths of one percent of respondents did not graduate from high school as compared to approximately twenty-four percent of white adults in the general population.[6]

---

5. Calculated by subtracting age at commitment to spiritual growth (question 34 on the survey) from their age at the time of the survey. Based on 1984 data.
6. Ibid.

Figure 8-By Education

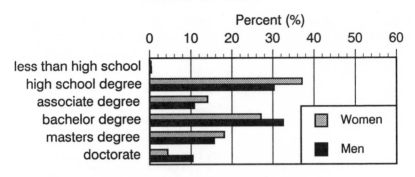

Figure 9 shows that about half of the respondents grew up in environments marked by some level of alcohol abuse.

Figure 9-As a Child, Around People Who Abused Alcohol

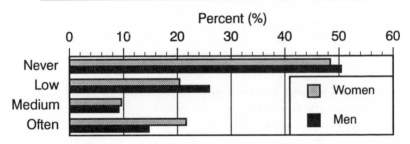

Figure 10 shows that about one-fifth of the respondents grew up in environments marked by some level of drug abuse (includes prescription drugs).

Figure 10-As a Child, Around People Who Abused Drugs

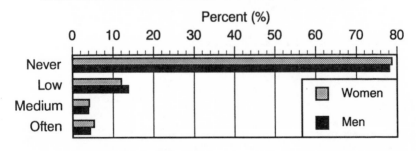

Figure 11 shows the status of the most recent relationship of each of those who responded. The married percentage (36%) is a little more than half that of the general population (63%).[7] One of the reasons cited for getting involved in New Age was to recover from a broken relationship. Through the interviews, I found that some people chose their spiritual growth over an existing relationship if there was a conflict. These two situations would contribute to the lower marriage percentages.

Figure 11-Most Recent Relationship

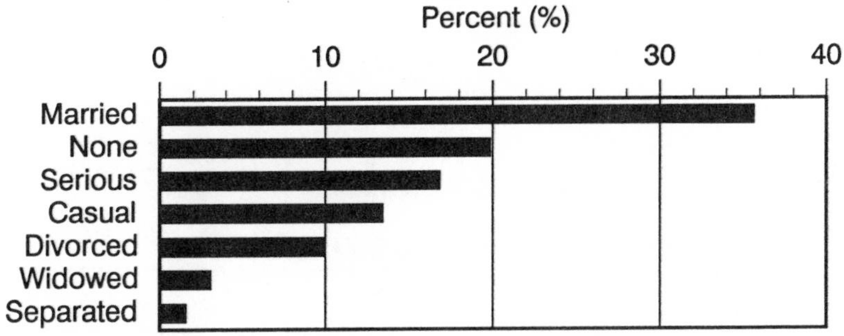

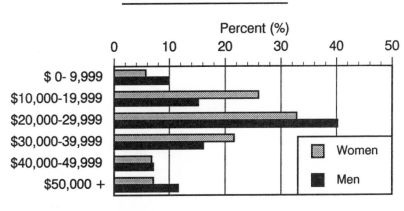

Figure 12 shows the breakdown in incomes listed on the surveys. Since some people listed household rather than their individual income, the results below include only the employed, unmarried respondents who included their income.

Figure 12-By Income Range

7. According to the 1989 *Statistical Abstract of the United States*, based on 1987 figures for the white population.

Figure 13 compares the differences in the number of people who were self-employed before and after their involvement in New Age. (Note: the statistics include only those people who were over 21 when they committed to their spiritual growth.) For women, the number is almost triple after involvement in New Age while the rate is more than double for men. That is consistent with their desire to take control of their lives and their willingness to take risks to find personal fulfillment. Often, the change to self-employment included a change in career according to the before and after occupations listed on the survey forms.

Figure 13-By Self-Employed

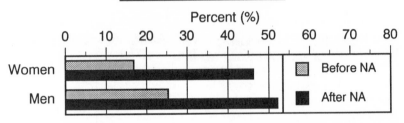

Figure 14 shows the current occupations of the respondents grouped by the author into the categories defined in the 1988-89 edition of the *Occupational Outlook Handbook* published by the U.S. Department of Labor. (Note: categories in italics were added by the author.)

Figure 14-By Current Occupation

Occupation Categories	Number	%
Managerial and Management Related	101	13.1%
Administrative Support and Clerical	90	11.7%
Writers, Artists, and Entertainers	90	11.7%
Service	65	8.5%
Teachers, Librarians, and Counselors	59	7.7%
RNs, Pharmacists, Dieticians, Therapists	54	7.0%
Marketing and Sales	48	6.2%
Retired	46	6.0%
Lawyers, Social and Religious Workers	36	4.7%
Health Technicians	29	3.8%
Technicians Other Than Health	29	3.8%
In Transition	21	2.7%
Students	18	2.3%
Construction	17	2.2%
Health Diagnosing and Treating Practitioners	13	1.7%
Engineers, Surveyors, and Architects	9	1.2%
Ill/Disabled	9	1.2%

Figure 14-By Current Occupation(Cont.)

Occupation Categories	Number	%
None	8	1.0%
Metaphysical	7	0.9%
Handlers, Helpers, Laborers	5	0.7%
Transportation	5	0.7%
Natural, Computer, and Mathematical Scientists	4	0.5%
Agriculture, Forestry, Fishing	3	0.4%
Mechanics, Installers, Repairers	3	0.4%
Military	0	0.0%
Miscellaneous	0	0.0%
Precision Production	0	0.0%

Figure 15 shows the percent of men and women by the reason for their involvement in New Age. The percentages total to more than one hundred percent because more than one reason could be given.

Figure 15-By Reason For Involvement

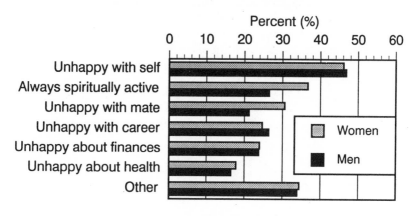

The major reasons included in the Other category are listed below in descending order by the number of times they were mentioned on the surveys:

- Illness/death of friend/relative
- Unhappy with some other aspect of life
- Looking for meaning in life, something is missing
- Following inner guidance
- Alcohol or drug abuse related
- Influence of books/TV/films

- Ending a relationship
- Psychedelic drug experience
- Psychic experience
- Accident/injury

For a more detailed breakdown of each Other category, see Appendix 2-Trigger Events.

Now we have a general picture of what a person involved in New Age looks like. They are mainly white, and three-quarters are women. Two-thirds are between the ages of thirty and fifty. Over two-thirds have a college degree, and over eighty percent come from a traditional religious background. Over half are married or in a serious relationship. Less than ten percent are only children. About half of them were exposed to some level of alcohol abuse as children and a fifth of them to some form of drug abuse. They are engaged in a wide variety of occupations, and many have become self-employed. They became involved in New Age as a result of a crisis or personal unhappiness, to continue an on-going spiritual search, or as a result of a spontaneous interest in their spiritual growth.

With that profile of a typical New Ager, we now move on to the personal stories where we will meet a variety of New Agers in the flesh and see what makes them each unique.

4 Introduction to Personal Stories

In the next three chapters, you will meet people at different stages in their spiritual journeys-some at high points and some at plateaus. Some have recently started while others have been traveling for decades. But each path is unique because each person's life experiences and personal goals are unique. Some have found certain books, workshops, or technologies to be helpful while others have drawn mainly on inner knowledge and resources. One thing that most of them have in common is that they are experiencing more peace and satisfaction than at any other time in their lives.

For those of you familiar with New Age, the stories may add to your collection of evidence of the growth and change that is possible for you. Or you may see someone whose struggles and triumphs you can identify with and increase your sense of connection with others.

For those of you who just want to learn about New Age, you will get a chance to look closely at several people involved in New Age. You will get an insight into their childhoods, their challenges in adulthood, their reasons for pursuing New Age thought, and its effect on their lives. Then you can reach your own conclusions about them and the trend they represent. You may even find something that can make a change in your own life if you're ready for it.

To get the most from the stories, quiet your desire to analyze and judge. Accept that these people are telling their life stories as they experienced them. If you do that, you will be open to a thought or insight that may help you resolve a problem in your own life. There is much you can take with you without threatening your own religious or spiritual beliefs.

If you are reading just to know more about New Age but don't want to get involved, that's fine too. The author appreciates your desire to learn.

The personal stories are divided into three major categories based on how each person became involved with New Age thought. The first category includes those people who were guided to New Age resources as a result of a crisis in their lives-often a bad relationship, illness, or death. The second category includes those people who found themselves drawn or guided to New Age ideas without an external crisis triggering them. The last category consists of people who have had some level of spiritual awareness most of their lives. At times it may have been suppressed, but they always felt they were searching for something. While some people may fit into more than one category, they were matched with the category that most directly influenced their contact with New Age thought.

The interviews contain each person's understanding of the books, teachings, and techniques they have explored. Others studying or teaching the same things may not agree with their interpretations. The purpose of the stories, however, is not to determine the accuracy of the beliefs each person holds but to understand what that person believes or how he interprets what he has studied.

You will find in the stories that many of the interviewees had negative experiences and attitudes regarding their childhood religions and often were the only one in the family who looked for other choices. Presenting their views is not meant as a condemnation of organized religion. Instead, it should be realized that those experiences and attitudes would be expected of people in a book about non-traditional spiritual paths. If they were still happy with their childhood religion, they wouldn't have been in a position to be included in this book.

Each of the stories contain most of the following subsections-Life Story, Life Goals, Parenting, Spiritual Beliefs, and Growth Techniques. Some also contain sections on Intuition, Reason, and Emotion; The Future; and an Update section at the end which includes information supplied by some interviewees several months after the original interview. In each section, the author has summarized the interviewee's related experiences, beliefs, and feelings and highlighted the summary by quotes from the interview. The author has not attempted to analyze or comment on the interviewee's story or beliefs. That process is left for each reader to do as he chooses. Names in the stories have been changed except in a few cases where people requested that their real names be used.

Readers are cautioned against reading all of the stories at once. They may be overwhelming to some people because of the many new concepts they contain and the possible conflict with the reader's existing ideas. One approach to reading the stories is to read the introduction to each of the next three chapters and determine what category most interests you. Each story in the chapters begins with a summary paragraph which you may use as a guide in selecting stories to read.

While the author was able to understand the experiences recounted in the interviews, she wasn't able to identify with most of them at that time. With each new reading and editing of the interviews, she found that she could identify with more of the experiences and beliefs because of similar experiences and realizations in her own life. After two and a half years and several rounds of editing the interviews, the author still gains more from each new reading and finds that something clicks that didn't before. If you are on a spiritual path, you may want to read the stories again after several months to see if you too have a different experience which you can credit to changes in yourself.

...an addiction is any desire that makes you upset or unhappy if it is not satisfied. Life is warning you to get rid of an addiction every time you are emotionally uncomfortable in any way.

- Handbook to Higher Consciousness

5   Growth Through Crisis

For each of these people, a personal crisis served as a catalyst for their introduction to New Age thought. The crisis may have been a failed relationship, a health problem, a death in the family, or a career problem. While similar crises may have happened before, most felt this one was too much. They were desperate for answers and their search lead them to New Age thought through books, seminars, counselors, or friends. Most look back on that crisis as a positive turning point in their life and now look at crises or problems as opportunities for growth rather than obstacles to be overcome.

Daniel (41, Jewish background, energy conservation manager)

Daniel has had an interest in healing since he was nine. After several years of marriage, he couldn't reconcile his outer success with his inner emptiness and depression. Concern for his health caused him to change his diet and to start exercising. Then he felt drawn to workshops on different forms of healing. He learned even more about healing and responsibility when he tried to help his father overcome a brain tumor.

Life Story
Daniel grew up in a Jewish community, but felt that his parents were involved only for the social aspects. He rebelled at what he thought was the hypocrisy of his parents' spirituality and never really embraced their religion.

Daniel became aware of his interest in healing at age nine when he was playing outside with his cousin who fell and skinned his knee. Daniel felt he should know what to do and was upset that he didn't, so he started reading everything he could about first aid. As a teenager, he taught first aid and water safety. And when he was old enough, he trained as an emergency medical technician (EMT) and volunteered on rescue squads as his way of reaching out to people.

Minutes before his first wedding, Daniel felt that the marriage wasn't right, but his concern for the guests made him go through with it. He and his wife lived in Brooklyn, close to where he worked as a high school shop teacher. *"All of Brooklyn's Jewishness is like a huge mother that keeps you from leaving the nest. It took years of small steps to get away."*

At twenty-eight, Daniel and his wife moved from Brooklyn and had a daughter the same year. *"I was scared out of my mind. I didn't feel ready for it. We were struggling as new parents in a new place."* Three years later, they owned a home, and while their lives looked stable, Daniel felt oppressed by the tension in his marriage.

At thirty-one, Daniel had a family, cars, job, and ambulance work, everything he thought he wanted. But while digging a post hole one day, he looked up and asked himself why he felt so awful. He had everything he wanted, and it meant nothing.

Then he injured his back doing some landscaping work, and his doctor painted a bleak picture about what he could expect about his back healing. But Daniel didn't accept his diagnosis and thought there must be something he could do for his back. So he searched the library and sought other resources to develop an exercise routine which slowly got his back into shape.

About the same time, Daniel was overcome with depression and scared by a loss of appetite and the ensuing weight loss. He asked himself how he could turn it into something positive. So he started researching nutritious foods in order to get the most benefit from his reduced appetite. He quickly became a vegetarian, which caused conflicts with his wife who didn't want to change her eating habits.

Then Daniel started another exercise program. The stretching exercises he did for his back led him to yoga and its associated philosophy, meditation, and diet. Then his yoga teacher suggested he try a massage. *"It was the first time I was touched by a woman other than a family member. It was a challenge to allow myself to be so vulnerable and to deal with my wife's unhappiness about it."* But Daniel noticed incredible changes in his body from those sessions.

Soon, Daniel was thin, strong, and muscular, looking like he did in college. *"I looked in the mirror and asked myself why I had covered that up."* Then Daniel started running, although he had never run before, not even as a child. He worked up slowly and became a fanatical runner.

While working on his physical body, Daniel started meditating. He said he began experiencing things that didn't make sense-seeing, feeling, and knowing things about other people. He was teaching disturbed children at the time, and he would suddenly know things that were troubling them, and he didn't know how he knew. Not knowing anyone who had had similar experiences, Daniel felt that he had to hide his own.

At a conference he attended with his wife, Daniel learned about an energy therapy technique called Therapeutic Touch, a technique similar to laying-on of hands. As Dr. Dolores Krieger explained the technique, Daniel began to understand what had been happening to him. The next day he went to a mini-workshop on the technique and later tried it on anyone who would stand still. He was excited when he made charley horses, sinus headaches, and bruises go away. He started taking other workshops on healing, including those based on Native American teachings and using crystals. But he started feeling isolated because no one he knew knew anything about what he was involved in. The contrast between the unhappiness of his marriage and the happiness he felt doing healing work pounded away at him. He began to go to workshops not only to learn, but to see how he felt about being close to other women.

Meanwhile, Daniel's father had moved to California after his wife died. He worked as a foster grandparent at a state school for retarded children and performed miracles for them by cutting through bureaucratic red tape to get what they needed. Daniel called his father on his birthday, and when his father didn't make sense on the phone, Daniel thought he had had a stroke. Later, a doctor diagnosed a brain tumor and wanted to operate. Daniel flew out immediately and did everything he knew to prepare his father for surgery, including energizing his father's IVs and meditating. His father was able to go home within ten days.

During the next year, Daniel's marriage fell apart. He had a short affair which resulted in a separation from his wife and mixed feelings of relief, guilt, and shame. His father visited and surprised Daniel when he asked him where he had gotten the courage to go ahead with the separation.

Soon after his father went back to California, Daniel called his father and noticed again that something was wrong with him. He called friends to take his father to the emergency room. A few weeks later, his father's nurse called to say his father was exhibiting paranoid behavior. Daniel dropped everything to go to his father's side. *"I meditated on the plane and heard a voice say I was going to learn about transition. I said 'OK.' Then the voice said, 'And reincarnation,' to which I responded, 'I'm not ready for that.' The voice said, 'Too bad, you're going to learn that too.'"*

Daniel went directly to the hospital and gave his father the best therapeutic session he had ever done. Daniel sensed the source of his father's paranoia and talked his father step by step through what had happened to him so he could understand where he was and why.

Being divorced by this time, Daniel planned to stay with his father as long as he needed him. His father decided not to take chemotherapy treatments for his tumor. When Daniel asked him if he was interested in any of the healing techniques he practiced, his father agreed to try them. So Daniel began looking for anyone he thought could heal his father, including a psychic surgeon and a Cherokee medicine man who was an expert with crystals.

But as the healers worked on his father, his condition slowly got worse. Then Daniel found a faith healer from a local church. As he watched her work on his father, he thought she could probably heal him, but he suddenly felt that his father didn't want to be healed. Daniel knew then that his father was going through the treatments for his sake. So he told the faith healer to stop.

Then Daniel knew the best thing he could do for his father was to prepare him to die. Over the next three weeks, his father's body went through a process of shutting down, and Daniel arranged for a hospice and a visiting nurse in case they were needed.

Daniel went to hear Elisabeth Kübler-Ross lecture on death and dying. She explained what would happen to Daniel's father and said everybody gets trained as they get ready to leave. She said no one has to help in preparations, but that each person does it himself. Finally, Daniel accepted that he wasn't responsible for his father any longer and concentrated instead on just taking care of him.

When his father had a seizure a few days later, Daniel called all the people who were on standby to help. Daniel wanted his father to understand his transition so he wouldn't be afraid. He could sense that his father was having out-of-body experiences, and he knew that his father was very comfortable when he was out of his body and uncomfortable when he was in it.

The next day Daniel called his aunt to tell her that his father was going to die soon and asked if she wanted to come and say good-bye. The next night, his father developed a strange breathing pattern that lasted until morning.

That day, his father's co-workers came to tell him that everyone missed him. *"The room filled up with all their love, and my father's breathing got very calm, and the whole room changed. But I changed into my old role as an EMT instead of a healer and checked my father's pulse instead of his energy."* His father's breathing and pulse slowed, and he seemed in a very peaceful state. Just then, Daniel saw his aunt walk past the picture window, and he saw the doorknob turn. As she walked into the room, his father died, as if he had waited as long as he could for her. He stayed with his father until he knew that the body wasn't his father any longer.

Two hundred people went to the service for Daniel's father, and one person after another stood and told stories about him, and his co-workers planted a tree for him. After the service, Daniel asked a friend to go with him to the tree that was planted in his father's memory so he could tell the tree about his father. The two of them sat by the tree and meditated for a while. When Daniel opened his eyes, the wind shifted and the tree seemed to bow to him. His friend asked if she saw what she thought she saw. Then the wind shifted ninety degrees and the tree bowed to her. Daniel said yes, she did, and they shook their heads and cried.

Daniel took a year's leave of absence and spent time studying Native American healing techniques and apprenticed in psychic surgery. He did Lifespring training and said he became a training junkie. He kept trying to "fix" himself. He worked in a psychiatric hospital and then as a spiritual healer in an emergency room. Then he went to Haiti for a few months to work with Mother Teresa's sisters, the Missionaries of Charity.

When he returned, he stayed with his aunt in New York for a while. *"I walked around the old neighborhood and felt as if I had dropped in from Mars. I saw a refrigerator crate and thought a family of four could live there. As I thought about what I had seen in Haiti, I was overwhelmed with how much we have in this country."* Through all his travels and experiences, Daniel was amazed that his needs for food and shelter were always met somehow.

Then Daniel moved to New England to stay with friends, eventually met his present wife, and took a teaching job at a psychiatric hospital. He learned that his ex-wife and daughter were having problems, so he and his wife agreed to take custody of his daughter. He said that taking a child in crisis into a new relationship has been quite a challenge for him and his wife.

He has taken a new job as a program manager and says he spends a lot of time on the phone talking to people who are confused or upset. He tries to make them feel good about themselves and the situations that are upsetting them. He is learning to use power with integrity. If he gets angry, he stops and asks himself why and what the underlying issue is.

Most of Daniel's and his wife's energy goes into being a new family, working on their house, and coping with his daughter's on-going crises. He said he's feeling things he never thought he would feel, particularly anger at his daughter. It's the biggest issue he has had to deal with in a long time.

He said he has no idea what the future will bring. Looking at his past, he could never have predicted what he would be doing a year in the future. He knows he can walk out the door and take care of himself, but he can't do that with a wife, daughter, house, and bills. Accepting that is something he is working on. And he expects to do spiritual healing again when the time feels right.

Update (September 1989)

Daniel wrote that his daughter had trouble adjusting to high school. *"Her anger and our reactions to it became overwhelming. I began to have chest pains and was tested for heart problems. It was just feeling brokenhearted."* His daughter went into foster care for a few months and then back to her mother, where her behavior seems to have improved.

Daniel was promoted at work, does a lot of work on the house, and has started doing healing again. *"Life is finally quieter, challenging, and full."*

Claire (55, Protestant background, in transition)

Claire grew up in a family with strong Victorian beliefs and addictive behavior. After stumbling onto metaphysical beliefs at age 49, Claire learned to channel spiritual teachers and recognized the addictive behavior of the members of her own family, including her own codependence. Her son's request for help with his addictions catapulted the whole family into therapy. After extensive work, Claire is discovering the joy of an intimate relationship with her husband for the first time in thirty-four years of marriage. As she heals herself, she finds the desire and strength to be of service to others.

Life Story

Claire's parents grew up in conservative Protestant religions, but they eventually gave up the church. Claire absorbed her parents' Victorian religious beliefs about sex and public behavior. They taught her to be a performer, to be successful, and to make other people happy. After college, she married, had three children, and worked as a teacher.

At age 49 she planned to open a new business using color analysis. In preparation, she went alone to a cabin to read a book about color healing and to develop her own philosophy about color. The book suggested using a pendulum to discover one's inner colors of healing.

Since Claire didn't know how to use a pendulum, she called her daughter for help. *"She suggested I rig one with my wedding ring and some string and told me how to recognize the different motions for yes and no answers."* Claire constructed her pendulum and asked if there were someone who could help her with her colors. The pendulum started moving, and Claire smelled the scent of roses and sensed another being in the room. The experience excited her, but turned her belief systems upside down. When her senses settled down, the world looked different. She suddenly felt sure there was life after death and that spirits existed that she couldn't see. Then she worked furiously with the pendulum, amazed at the amount of information she discovered with yes and no questions.

When Claire returned home, she cancelled all of her appointments for the week and spent the time asking questions with her daughter and youngest son. *"We also learned a lot from my three month-old grandchild who saw things we couldn't. We all felt different energies around us."*

Later, Claire and members of her family learned to channel spirits. Claire began channeling for clients who wanted clarity about certain areas of their lives. This new business venture thrilled Claire, but she didn't realize that she was avoiding looking at problems in her own life.

A few years later, Claire read several books about codependence and addictions and realized she had grown up in a dysfunctional family. Her parents didn't drink, but she saw their Victorian view of sex as addictive.

A month later, her son called from college to ask for help with his addictions to marijuana and alcohol. Claire and her husband sent him to a treatment center where the whole family joined him in treatment for family week. Claire's husband recognized how his drinking had influenced his son and he stopped. Claire's addictions were codependency, smoking, and drinking. She defined her codependency as a need to be in control of herself and others by saying, *"I'll do it myself."*

Claire said she and her husband learned that they had failed their son by not setting boundaries for him so that he could learn the consequences of his behavior. They decided to start then by tying their son's college money to his keeping away from drugs and alcohol. When he admitted slipping a few times the next year, they stopped the money since he had used it to support his addictions. She said her son is on his own, responsible for his own life, and finally growing up.

In the year before the interview, Claire's family spent considerable time and money treating their addictions and participating in each other's family week of treatment. Claire stopped channeling because she thought she wouldn't be clear and balanced enough to be an effective channel for her clients during her recovery.

Through the addiction therapy and treatment, Claire learned that she had to supplement her spiritual work with learning to feel her feelings and expressing them. She used to think that she could work on all of her problems from a spiritual perspective. But working on relationships with her birth family (parents and siblings) has been critical to her healing.

During treatment, Claire discovered she had been a victim of incest. A spiritual healer tried to guide her toward forgiveness, but she wasn't ready. She thought it might be several months before she could do that. A year earlier she would have tried to forgive, but now she feels that if the lower chakras[1] aren't ready for forgiveness, she could harm herself by pretending. And she doesn't want to betray her inner child again.

Claire feels as if she is learning to walk again, to be new in the world in every way. And she is learning how to be in a truly intimate relationship for the first time after thirty-four years of marriage. Claire and her family are doing well, able now to recognize and change their addictive patterns.

Life Goals

Claire wants to live and model a healthy life, free from the tyranny of addiction. She wants to stay in each moment, painful or joyous, accept all of herself, and be of service. She used to think that being of service meant helping others, assuming she knew what was right for them. Now it means helping when she is asked. She trusts that people will come to her for help if and when they want it.

To prepare for her next career, Claire has earned a masters degree in counseling and has interned in psychodrama therapy. She hopes to direct a psychodrama group at a treatment center because it was so effective for her.

Sometimes she wonders if she should stop work on herself to dash out to citizen summit meetings. But she feels that she needs another year of therapy in order to be effective in the world. She knows she has to listen to herself to know what is right for her. If she rushes out to do things because of outside pressure, she isn't being true to herself, and she's letting others control her. In the meantime, she writes and sends telegrams to politicians about issues she feels strongly about.

Spiritual Beliefs

Claire said she wouldn't want to be alive without her spiritual beliefs. Her friends include people with similar beliefs and people recovering

---

1. According to Eastern esoteric literature, chakras are energy centers in the body related to different physical, mental, emotional, or spiritual aspects of the body. The lower chakras are related to fear, anger, sexual issues, and personal power.

from addiction. *"Some of my friends involved in spiritual pursuits but not addiction therapy don't understand the time and energy I put into that. I explain to them my need to care for the child within whom I ignored for so many years."*

Claire has a sense of God being outside as well as inside her. She appreciates meeting God through the twelve step programs, although her concept of God still shifts and changes. But she knows that when she turns problems over to God, her life goes well. When her codependent urges arise, she reminds herself to turn her life and will over to God.

Claire believes the purpose of life is to grow so that one can return to God. *"I have received that message many times in channeling, and I see the human experience as a wonderful opportunity for enormous leaps in growth."*

Growth Techniques

Claire learned much about herself and what needed to be healed from the channeled messages of her spiritual teachers. And most of her growth and healing has come from addiction therapy. She wonders if there is a correlation between people who channel and people who come from addictive backgrounds, whom she thinks developed extrasensory abilities to cope with their dysfunctional family. She thinks channeling may be a natural extension of something that develops in childhood as a survival tool.

Claire follows a daily ritual with her husband to stay focused on growth and healing:

- One half hour aerobic walk in the morning
- Meditating for fifteen minutes
- Taking turns praying aloud so that each can hear what is going on with the other
- Saying how they feel and their affirmation for the day
- Short readings from an inspirational book
- Body work (massage, rolfing[2], or polarity therapy[3])

"When I don't follow the above routine, I feel irritable and out of balance later in the day. If this is an addiction, I love it."

Claire also belongs to a group that meets once a month to socialize, "recharge their batteries," and meditate. The group includes people involved in Soviet-American peace talks, university teachers, and students.

---

2. Rolfing. A series of bodywork sessions which aim for structural alignment and balance through deep tissue manipulation. The process was founded by Ida P. Rolf.
3. Polarity therapy was developed by Dr. Randolph Stone and consists of light touch, stretching exercises, and nutritional guidelines whose goal is to balance the body's electromagnetic energy.

She sees obstacles as inside herself and works hard at clearing them by using transactional analysis, reparenting, and working with the adult, child, and parent aspects of herself.

Update (August 1989)

A month after the interview, Claire started directing psychodrama at a treatment center part time and loves it. *"Our whole family continues our recovery process. It's slow but pretty steady. Life is good."*

Allison (36, Baptist background, teaches blind children)

Allison survived encephalitis, oppressive religious training, and parents who never expected her to succeed. She surprised everyone by achieving her childhood dream of teaching blind children. The cumulative effects of her family, church life, and her first marriage nearly stilled her inner voice and had stolen her self-esteem. After Allison's divorce, she found a counselor who helped her accept herself and rediscover her inner guidance.

Life Story

When she was only a few days old, Allison developed encephalitis and was the only child treated for it in the area that year who didn't die. When her parents told her about it later, their sadness caused Allison to feel guilty that she had survived.

Allison said her parents always viewed her as a sick child, even after she recovered. Her mother told her she was retarded and would have mental problems. As a child, she accepted what her parents said and viewed herself as they did. Yet part of her didn't believe they were right.

Allison's parents were Presbyterian, but didn't go to church when Allison was a child. They did, however, drop Allison and her brother off at the Baptist church for Sunday school. *"I'm not sure if my mother realized what kind of training I was getting or if she thought all Protestant training was the same. I wondered why my parents brought me to a church where people said that Jesus loved me and then yelled at me for being a sinner. I found myself doing things out of fear of going to hell rather than because they made me feel good."*

Allison remembered a Sunday school teacher telling her that if she set foot in any church other than the Baptist church, God would strike her down with lightning. Many years later, that fear kept her from going to her husband's church and kept her from exploring other religious alternatives.

As a child, Allison was interested in metaphysical topics. She had books on ESP and reincarnation that she hid from her church friends. She said the information in them created a foundation that she began to build on many years later.

After seeing the movie, *The Miracle Worker,* at age nine, Allison decided she would teach blind children when she grew up. She even picked out the town in which she wanted to teach. She often talked about it and made plans to accomplish it. Friends and family were skeptical and tried to change her mind, and her parents thought she should pursue her musical talents. Her mother didn't think she could make it through college. Even though Allison never doubted her dream, she said she had to work extra hard to achieve it because she had such a low self-image.

Allison said she has always been aware of an inner voice and inner energy that gives her ideas and points her in certain directions. *"When I was a child, the voice was loud, but when I followed it, my mom or teachers would squash it down. When it happened several times, I learned that following it could be socially unacceptable. Since I didn't want to rock the boat, I began to doubt my voice."*

Allison stopped going to church in high school. *"I never set foot in the Baptist church again. I never felt it was a church of love. The fact that my parents didn't go made it harder because I couldn't talk to them about what I was learning. I learned Christian values that were helpful to me, but I didn't feel good about organized religion."*

Allison had a mystifying experience in tenth grade while playing volleyball. While watching for the ball, Allison saw the scene change before her eyes from the gym to a view of the universe. *"I felt a part of it and felt an overwhelming sense of love and understanding of the universe. Suddenly I saw the gym class again, and I started shaking and wondered, 'What the hell was that.' I wanted the experience to come back because that was where I wanted to be. I didn't tell anyone because I thought I was losing my mind. After all, my parents thought I was retarded. But I realized I had a feeling in that one second that I never had in all those years of sitting in church."*

Four years later, a college religion class helped Allison to understand her experience when she read about mystical experiences. She learned that they come on a person suddenly, the person experiences well-being and oneness with the universe, and the person can't explain the experience in words. She saw her experience as a "window opening on another reality." She wants to get back to that place again and believes that's where she'll go when she dies.

As a teenager, Allison began to prepare herself for her teaching role by working with blind children at the YMCA. As she taught them, she noticed her own self-confidence and inner strength growing. She realized that she needed to get away from her parents' limited expectations of her.

Allison earned college scholarships and was sure she was on the right path when she found no resistance to her plans. In graduate school, the variety and openness of ideas excited her, and she found it hard to go back home to her parents' view of her as a sick child. She moved away from her parents and sees them only a few times a year. A network of friends she has developed over the years has become her new family.

After a few years of teaching, Allison had achieved all the material and career goals she had set for herself, but felt increasingly unhappy and didn't know why. She heard the outside world telling her she should get married and have a family in addition to her career. *"I started listening more to the outside 'shoulds' than my own inner light."*

Allison began seeing a counselor to discuss issues about love, independence, and children that were coming up for her as she began dating the man who would become her husband. *"I hadn't met anyone like my counselor before, who listened without judgement or voicing limiting thoughts. She helped me see that I was OK and nurtured the little girl in me which helped me to grow again. I've always felt that she provided the missing parts of parenting for me. She introduced me to new ideas and got me thinking along a spiritual path in a way that wasn't threatening to me."* Allison's counselor also taught her the techniques of reframing[4] and visualization to help her take charge of her life. *"When I get stuck on something, I almost physically shift how I look at it to see another point of view or to get a new insight."*

Allison eventually married and enjoyed having someone to share her life with. But after a few years, she felt she had stopped growing as a person and felt pulled down by her husband's negative attitudes. Even as she did everything she thought a wife should do to please her husband, she felt her inner light get dimmer. She didn't understand why she didn't feel good about her life and her job when she felt she was doing what society expected of her.

After five years of marriage, Allison's husband told her that he was leaving her for another woman. Allison was stunned when the person she had been living for left. She felt her identity ripped from her, leaving her empty inside.

Allison had suffered from agoraphobia, or fear of open places, in the past. After her husband left, her agoraphobia intensified and she didn't

---

4. Reframing is a psychological technique used to look at situations from different perspectives.

go out of her house for a month. She developed an eating disorder, resulting in significant weight loss, and for a while, she used alcohol as an escape from her confusion and emptiness.

But she felt the little ball of energy inside her getting stronger and telling her everything was all right. She began to consciously tune into her inner light, ready to trust the magnet in her to point her in the right direction. *"When the right thoughts came through, I felt the ball inside me get bigger and start to vibrate, and I felt an energy force around me."*

Her inner voice led her to music as an aid to her recovery. Allison had been involved with music all of her life except during her marriage because her husband wasn't interested in it. She knew she could nurture herself with it. And once she started giving to herself, she found she had more to give to her students, and she enjoyed her job again.

In addition to her teaching job, Allison played music five hours a day and felt a tremendous release of energy. She started to meet people who helped her feel good about herself. She used affirmations to set her sights on a part-time job as a keyboardist for a rock group and was excited when she got it.

After her divorce, Allison had to reevaluate her future because she felt she had done everything she was supposed to do. She looked for the parts of herself that she should throw away and those that she should keep. As she listened to herself, Allison was unhappy with the judgmental part that made her feel guilty. She began to look at each experience as a learning experience to be observed and stored for later reference rather than judged.

The guilt Allison felt about surviving encephalitis gave way to acceptance of herself as a baby who had a strong will to live. When she feels depressed, she remembers that she has something inside her that keeps her going. Allison also knows that her brain was not damaged by the disease and realizes that she carried anger around most of her life because she listened to her parents instead of her inner self.

She finally feels ready for another relationship and visualizes the kind of person she is looking for. She knows he is out there and that her only chance to find him is to believe she will.

Since her divorce, Allison has developed a new set of friends who support and understand her spiritual needs. *"A couple of others about my age seem to be so much further along. And I don't get the feeling that it's from this life."* She learns a lot from them and from her students, some of whom she senses have a level of experience and awareness that they also must have come into this world with.

Allison continues to use affirmations and is excited when they turn into reality. And she continues to listen to her inner guidance. *"Before my divorce, I listened a lot to outside sources and put up barriers to my own inner answers. When I listened to outside 'shoulds' or 'should nots,' that's when I got into trouble. I feel a lot more secure now listening to my own inner guidance."*

Her agoraphobia still causes Allison some anxiety which is why she takes extra time in the morning to prepare for the day and to get herself out of the house. She worked with her counselor on it and has only sporadic attacks now.

Finding the time and energy for everything she wants to do is getting harder. Because her music helps to energize her, she is already down to four hours sleep per night and takes short naps during the day to keep going.

Spiritual Beliefs

Allison believes each person is capable of making decisions for his or her life. Each moment in life has a yes or no choice. Each choice determines the next path. She believes that two people can get to the same point by different paths. She helps people look at options they have, but she won't make decisions for them.

Allison's path involves talking and listening to people and knowing she isn't alone. Then she listens to herself. For her, life is a journey that doesn't end at death. Seeing how much she has changed in only two years makes her eager to see where she will be in ten years.

Allison worked hard on her ability to look at life positively so that it has become almost natural for her. Now she looks with gratitude at her experiences for the opportunities they gave her to strengthen her abilities to deal with people. She works at being open about what she feels and prefers to influence people by example rather than words.

Allison views God as a force in the universe that has guidelines and rules but has not set her fate.

Eastern religions interest Allison because of their lack of emphasis on good and bad. Seeing life as a learning experience is a belief that she feels serves her better.

She has read about witchcraft, pagan religions and the persecution by the church. She believes the devil is a concept created by the church to get rid of old thought and to scare people into thinking the church's way. *"I don't think there is 'bad' out there. There are just experiences, some less pleasant than others. I believe in yin and yang energies which balance each other but not that one is inherently evil and the other good."*

Growth Techniques

Allison credits her counselor as having the greatest influence on her by nurturing the child in her and listening without judging or setting limits on her.

Keeping momentum going day after day is a challenge. Depression is still hard for Allison to keep at bay. If she's alone too long and starts to feel down, she calls friends for help.

Allison sees her growth coming through working with small groups of people. *"I'm not a global person; I'm a front-line person."* Working with the blind teaches her new ways to look at people and things and has taught her that sometimes vision can block someone from seeing people as they really are.

She finds that people usually introduce her to books that are right for her at the time.

The Future

For a long time, Allison was concerned about the threat of nuclear war. She feels that technology is growing faster than our maturity to use it properly. Pollution concerns her, but she doesn't expect any changes until a major problem occurs. *"It may result in a lot of deaths before a solution is found. We'll just squeak by dealing with each problem or symptom rather than working on prevention. I can't think too much about the future because it's so overwhelming. I just try to chip away at the little pieces that are within my reach."*

Monica (22, Catholic background, government worker)

Having a father in the Air Force resulted in Monica's family moving often and created a lonely childhood for her. As an introverted teen, she became depressed and overweight. On the verge of suicide at nineteen, Monica found a therapist who helped build her self-esteem and gave her reasons to stay in the world.

Life Story

Finding it hard to make friends because her family moved so often, Monica looked for support in the Catholic church where she thought she would find acceptance from the other children. When she didn't, her faith in the church was shaken.

The Catholic church had told her what to believe, what to do, and not to question. But she did question the beliefs that seemed so harsh. She found contradictions in the Bible that she couldn't resolve. Her Sunday school teachers told her to take the teachings on faith, but she couldn't accept that. She felt the church was teaching one philosophy, but using another. And she felt the Church's attitude towards women was oppressive.

Monica was thirteen when her family finally stopped moving. By then she had poor relationships with family members and spent most of the time in her room. Monica's parents continually compared her to her older sister, who was popular and did well in school. *"I was depressed because I didn't measure up. I began to wonder why life was so unfair. I was unhappy all the time and gained a lot of weight in high school."* Monica began to withdraw from people and only went out if her sister went with her.

When Monica graduated from high school, she stopped going to church and had no idea what to do with her life. Her self-esteem was at its lowest point. Even as she gained fifty more pounds, she longed for people to see past her weight and accept her as she was. She said her father was emotionally and verbally abusive because he disliked "fat" women. Monica felt more humiliated by his taunts and jokes than by all of her peers put together. She felt abandoned and rejected by him.

At nineteen, Monica made plans to commit suicide, but some part of her that wanted to live prompted her to call a therapist. *"The therapist helped me to see that I'm a competent, worthwhile person and that I can create the life I want. I knew she was there to help me. When one of my aunts died during that time, I had to examine my beliefs about death and dying because I didn't believe everything I had been taught in church anymore."* The therapist suggested some books for Monica, including Raymond A. Moody's *Life After Life*, the Seth[5] books, and books by Elisabeth Kübler-Ross.[6] Monica found comfort in their philosophy about life and life after death.

Her therapist used the concepts in the books to discuss Monica's thoughts of suicide. She suggested that each person is here to learn certain lessons and to teach other lessons as well. If Monica doesn't learn everything she is supposed to in this life, the therapist said she may have to try again in the next one. Monica began looking at her mistakes or problems as learning experiences instead of worrying about them and feeling she had failed.

For a while, Monica felt guilty about abandoning the religion that had been such a big part of her life. She wasn't sure she would ever feel spiritually fulfilled even with her therapist's help. But she felt it was time to move beyond "the restrictive teachings" of the church. She said if she

---

5. Seth is a non-physical entity or energy personality who channeled several metaphysical books through Jane Roberts starting in the late 1960's.
6. Dr. Elisabeth Kübler-Ross is an internationally recognized expert in the field of death and dying.

were not meant to be where she is, her Higher Power wouldn't have brought her there.

Monica's therapist suggested that she write short and long-term goals and complete at least one to give her a sense of accomplishment. Not long before the interview for this book, Monica completed a train trip by herself, which surprised her family. Her mother told her she was proud of her new found independence.

Monica is also working on her weight by dieting and exercising. She is using a workbook titled *Making Peace With Food,* by Susan Kano, which addresses beliefs people have about food and body image. *"As I begin to accept my body, I see it slowly changing. My therapist also had a weight problem and is especially supportive."*

Monica continues to grow, read, and explore. She started working, is finally making friends, and enjoys going places on her own. Through counseling, she discovered reasons for her depression that she had been suppressing, including being sexually abused as a child by a family acquaintance. She's no longer ashamed of what happened because she knows it wasn't her fault. She plans to continue seeing her therapist to work on that and other issues.

Monica sees several career possibilities for herself. She is considering going to school to become a teacher or a therapist. Or she may start her own business. Monica plans to move out of her parents' house and to develop supportive relationships by being more open with people. Whether they accept her or not, she holds onto the thought that she is a capable, caring person.

Monica has made improvements in her relationship with her father during the past year, making it clear she won't accept his abuse. She has offered several times to start over with him, but he hasn't been interested. So she is trying to accept that and move on.

Spiritual Beliefs

"In the Catholic church, there is a lot of emphasis on guilt, being a sinner, self-sacrifice, and doing the right thing by society's standards. I think taking care of myself is not selfish, but instead is essential to my survival. I used to be a sucker for helping everyone else to the detriment of myself."

Monica said that the concept of being a sinner and feeling guilty for making mistakes resulted in her low self-esteem, and she won't accept that for herself anymore. But she's still trying to overcome her desire to control the actions of others to keep them from doing things she thinks may hurt them. She wants to respect their freedom to learn from their mistakes so that she can expect the same freedom.

Monica has stopped using male-oriented words from the Catholic church, including "God." She calls her source of strength her Higher Power, and she doesn't want a "middle man" to help her talk to it. Even though she declines to go to church with her friends, she respects their spiritual choices and believes there is more than one "right" path.

A major change from her Catholic beliefs is that a spiritual person can have abundance in her life, an attitude which relieves her worry about where her next dollar is coming from.

Growth Techniques

Monica highly recommends therapy, if appropriate, as a tool for growth. She said that some religious groups are against any therapy that isn't part of their teachings, and some consider it brainwashing. *"But it's not going to change your mind about anything unless you want it to change. If one counselor or type of therapy isn't working for you, try another. Always remember that you have choices no matter what the situation."*

Monica had kept a journal for a few years before counseling, and her therapist recommended she continue with it, focusing on recording her thoughts and feelings. *"When I'm feeling down, I can go back and read past entries that show me coming out of a similar depression. It helps me keep a good outlook on life and reassures me that things can and will go well for me."*

Her therapist taught her meditation and relaxation techniques in order to reduce anxiety and everyday stress. And Monica has started practicing yoga for her health and creative visualization for her goals.

She has special appreciation for the following books:

• *Codependent No More* by Melody Beattie. *"It took me two weeks to read it even though it's a small book because almost everything Beattie mentioned about unhealthy and destructive relationships described my relationships, and that hurt."*

• *Life after Life* by Raymond A. Moody.

• *Creative Visualization* by Shakti Gawain.

• The Seth books, especially *The Education of Oversoul, No. 7*.

Update (June 1989)

In May 1989, Monica was shaken by the death of a good friend, and in June 1989 she was waiting to hear if she was going to be laid off her job. As she reviewed the transcript of the interview during that time, she said she was reminded of how much she had to be thankful for. *"I know my faith is being tested, and I also believe I've passed the test because I'm in pretty good spirits, and I still feel life is worth living."*

Diane (41, Protestant background, nutrition counselor)

Diane (real name) attributes years of illness to her thymus being irradiated when she was a child. Her search for health led her to alternative health practitioners. As she regained her health, her drive to find her life's mission was so strong that she divorced her husband and left her children to work and study with a spiritual teacher. Five years later, she is back with her children, working at a job she loves, and creating healthy relationships.

Life Story

As a child, Diane went regularly with her mother to the Methodist church for the social activities, but her father didn't attend church. When Diane was seven, her family moved to a small town and went to the Congregationalist church. Because it had limited social activities, Diane and her mother didn't go as regularly. Diane's mother stopped going to church when her parents died, but Diane continued going during high school and college. *"I'm glad I was exposed to religion without being forced to go against my will. I think it helped lay groundwork for the spiritual exploration I've done since."*

Diane's thymus was irradiated when she was a child because a doctor found it to be enlarged. Diane said at the time doctors didn't understand the connection between the thymus and the immune system and that a large thymus was not really a problem. She attributes years of health problems to the effect of the radiation on her thymus.

After college, Diane worked as an engineer. After marrying and having two children, she quit work to take care of her family. A few years later, her husband was transferred to a town in Florida, which Diane later found had a reputation as a spiritually aware community.

Meanwhile, she had seen many doctors about her health problems. Most of them told her that her problems were part of getting older and that she would have to learn to live with them. Her son's nursery school teacher recommended a chiropractor who taught Diane biofeedback and body awareness. Diane learned to raise the temperature of her thyroid, enabling her to reduce her thyroid medicine. The biofeedback process helped her learn to enter a theta brain wave state which she said made her creative visualizations about her health very effective.

While waiting in line in a department store, she met a woman who recommended a chiropractor for Diane's son, who has cerebral palsy. The chiropractor also helped Diane finally overcome her thyroid problem with a cranial adjustment, allowing her to stop her thyroid medication.

Diane continued to explore alternative health practices since conventional medicine had failed her. Shortly after moving to Florida, she had a dream that she would work with nutrition. Three years later, she opened a health food store and has educated herself in health and nutrition ever since.

When Diane was diagnosed with heart valve problems, a doctor told her the problems might be related to a thought that her husband didn't love her. That was her first exposure to the concept that emotional issues can be related to health problems. Diane realized that she hadn't let her husband love her.

Once her health improved, Diane's spiritual interests began tugging at her. Her passion to find her mission in life became so overwhelming that she divorced her husband, left her children with him, and moved to another city to study with a spiritual teacher to whom she felt drawn. *"Until then, I hadn't felt very alive. It was like the volume on my life was turned down so low that I didn't know what I was missing. Now I'm always aware of what is missing. And I have to guard against being satisfied with areas of my life that aren't what I want."*

She worked for several years with her spiritual mentor to learn tools to discover what she wanted from life and how to create it. *"When I come up against spiritual walls, people with similar spiritual goals and values come along to help me, and I usually end up shifting my perspective."* One goal led to her administering a nutrition program under a doctor's supervision.

In the future, Diane plans to pay more attention to her own standards and integrity than to external standards even though she risks rejection. When she comes to the end of her life, she wants to feel that she did most of what she came here to do. She wants to discover and reach her potential and to enjoy the process.

Spiritual Beliefs

Diane lives each day based on the belief that she invents everything that happens in her life. She tries not to blame what goes wrong in her life on someone else. Instead, she looks for what she can learn or what she should change in her life.

Her concept of God evolves continually. *"I believe people are all pieces of a mirror which holds God's reflection. Each person acts as a mirror to each other person and can see the reflection of God in himself and others. God is the completeness that I am not. I can only hope to experience God, not be God. The expression of God's spirit through me is unique. I'm a unique piece of the puzzle, and all of the pieces add up to God.*" When people mirror things that make her feel uncomfortable, Diane looks for what they are reflecting in her life.

Diane struggles over the concept of divine will versus free will. *"If people submit to divine will, do they become robots? If so, what is the purpose of living? As I understand God's system, I can ask for what I want (free will), but I can't specify how it will be filled (divine will). You get what you want, but you aren't sure how it will happen."*

Growth Techniques

Diane credits the tools she learned from her spiritual mentor to help "invent her life" as important assets in her spiritual growth.

Books that had a powerful influence on her were those by Darwin Gross, Paul Twitchell, and Shakti Gawain.

For nine years, she has taken quiet time each day to find insights into herself and her life. Insights may come during the contemplation or later in the day.

If someone wants to change her life, Diane would tell her, *"Take a hard look at your life. Are you happy? Would you do what you're doing if you had unlimited time and money? What are you most afraid of or concerned about? What would it take to do what you wanted in spite of your fears?"*

Evaluating her life and facing her fears has been the hardest part of her own growth process. But she says she is sick or stressed only when she procrastinates about dealing with a fear, concern, or limiting belief. She says she has more fun in the long run when she faces them and decides to leave them behind.

Update (August 1989)

Since the interview, Diane has moved back to Florida to be with her children and parents and to pursue her goal of bringing the concept of "inventing" to corporations. She is working as an engineer and said she is one of the few people she knows who wouldn't quit her job if she won the Florida lottery. And she has "invented" her perfect relationship helping to complete the balance in her life that she has sought for so long.

Bonnie (37, Lutheran background, artist/bartender)

Bonnie had a happy, normal childhood and a very successful corporate career. But after a few years, she realized the sacrifices she had made for it. She developed a fear of flying and used drugs and alcohol to fight the anxiety. A metaphysical bookstore became the catalyst for major changes in her life, including quitting her job and learning to tend bar so she could support her newfound talent as an artist.

Life Story

Bonnie went to the Lutheran church every Sunday until she was eighteen, her social life centering around it. When Bonnie left home, she stopped going to church regularly because she felt she could connect with God anywhere.

Bonnie started work with a large electronics company in 1982. She had five promotions in six years and tripled her salary. But her job required transfers to different cities. After a transfer to Texas, Bonnie realized how much she had given up for her career, especially being near her family. Deciding that happiness was more important than her job, she checked into career opportunities in Atlanta. A month later, her boss asked her if she would be interested in transferring there. She was amazed at the coincidence and happily accepted the offer.

Bonnie still traveled often in her job and began feeling lonely. She developed a fear of flying after enjoying it for twenty years and started using pills and alcohol to calm herself before getting on a plane.

A year later, after winning several sales awards, Bonnie's new boss told her that she didn't have a strong enough technical background for her job. She said he tried to drive her out of his department, but she wouldn't leave.

During lunch one day, she noticed a metaphysical book store and stopped in and stayed for three hours. She said the books, crystals, and energy in the store mesmerized her. She began going several times a week and used most of her spare time to read. Then she noticed an emptiness and loneliness she hadn't felt before.

She realized she had been unhappy for a long time. Money seemed unimportant. She thought she should be doing something else with her life but didn't know what. With all of her traveling, she didn't feel as if she had a life. *"There are more important things in life than spending it in a hotel room, living out of a suitcase with unreasonable demands put on you continually. As soon as you exceed them, they want more and more."* When Bonnie got her next promotion, she asked herself what part of her the company would buy next. She wondered why living the American dream of success left her feeling so unhappy and empty.

Bonnie's sister suggested she find a hobby to give her some enjoyment. She decided to take a drawing course and was amazed at what she could do. But she still felt something was missing.

A few months later, Bonnie met a young woman at the metaphysical bookstore with whom she felt an instant connection. Bonnie seemed to run into her every time she went to the store. One Saturday her friend introduced her to another woman who was starting a metaphysical art school and suggested that Bonnie attend. Bonnie was skeptical about her abilities but decided to trust her friend's instincts and started the class the next week.

In her first class, Bonnie applied a base coat of paint to her canvas and soon noticed the faint outline of a face and called the instructor over. The instructor said that was common with people who were psychic and worked with Bonnie to bring the face out in more detail. When Bonnie finished, most of the people in the class recognized the face as their image of a spirit. Bonnie was stunned by what she had produced. But she didn't try painting again for over a week because she was afraid nothing would happen. But the next time she painted, she saw a face again. So she started painting more and began to trust her ability and to enjoy the experience.

Bonnie's job became an obstacle that kept her from doing what she truly wanted. She began to search for information that explained her painting, such as channeling without going into a trance. Her painting became the most fulfilling part of her life. Her happiness made her more tolerant and patient with people at work. *"I came to the conclusion that when you die, what you did is not going to be as important as the way you did it."*

On a business trip, Bonnie's boss asked her to lie to a customer. She refused and flew home, glad to discover her limits regarding money. But something died in her that day. Leaving work wasn't a major decision anymore; the only questions were when and how would she make a living.

After Bonnie's boss transferred and she earned another promotion, Bonnie felt she had nothing left to prove at work and quit a few months later. To temporarily support herself, Bonnie took a bartending course and works nights so she can practice and explore her painting during the day.

When Bonnie wakes up, she usually has a feeling that tells her if she is going to paint that day. When the time is right during the day, she knows it. She has trouble saying thank you for compliments on her art because she believes her paintings are more the result of God's energy than her own abilities. She isn't sure where her painting will take her, but she trusts that God will give her the guidance she needs.

Today, Bonnie works at accepting responsibility for her life. When her concerns about finances arise, she reminds herself to trust that her needs will be met. She also tries to strike a balance between discernment and judgment especially concerning people's motives. While she tries to listen to her inner voice, her mind and survival instinct often drown it out. *"It's hard to let go and let it be easy."*

Life Goals

Bonnie feels strongly that she has a mission and takes her religion and spirituality very seriously. *"Revelations says believe and spread the word. I think that can mean showing or doing something for someone rather than preaching. I want to always be able to look in the mirror and say I'm the kind of person I like. I'm the only one who has to be happy with me."*

Spiritual Beliefs

Bonnie feels a close connection to God when she paints. She feels He is taking a personal interest in her art and she has a greater appreciation of Him. She prays to God for help, peace of mind, happiness, and guidance to stay on track.

Bonnie evaluates her actions based on her compassion and love for others rather than the karma that may result. Someone who hurts another is wrong, she says, because that person hurts himself since everyone is connected.

Bonnie feels that God presents Himself in whatever way can be accepted by a person. She thinks of God as a never ending source of energy. *"God's energy is what allows you to do what you do in this life. I saw a friend die at work two years ago, and I had the impression that an energy left his body. Suddenly, he had no electricity, no vibration. I see God as that electrical energy that you can see, feel, and know. It's everywhere. When it isn't there, you know it."*

The purpose of life, Bonnie says, is for each person to travel on his road to perfection and truth. *"Life on this earth is like going to school. Every time you come back, you learn something new. God has his purpose for our lives. He has arranged this whole thing. And I know the answer is deep inside me because I've made choices in my life based on that purpose."*

Bonnie said her religious beliefs haven't changed much because she has always had some beliefs that didn't agree with her church's teachings. Her religion has always been very personal to her and doesn't involve preaching to others. She was influenced by a grandmother who was a healer and her mother who has psychic abilities.

Bonnie focuses on herself and her growth. *"If I can't get there, how can I help someone else? We all have to get there ourselves. Each person has to change for the world to change. It happens through an evolution of people's attitudes. Take care of the little things and the big things will take care of themselves."*

Growth Techniques

Bonnie uses crystals to change the vibration of her home and to influence her energy. She uses them in prayer and to awaken old memories. A moonstone in her paint box helps her generate creativity. She became interested in crystals after visiting the metaphysical bookstore and attributing the peaceful atmosphere to the crystals on display. She said, however, that she isn't superstitious or dependent on them.

Eileen (45, Catholic background, customer service manager)

Eileen stopped going to Church at fifteen and realized she was gay at eighteen. Her attraction to metaphysics, twenty-five years later, grew out of a need to forgive herself and to deal with a sense of loss in her life. She found what she was looking for at Shirley MacLaine's Higher Self seminar and by participating in a local spiritual center.

Life Story

Eileen's parents were practicing Catholics, but she didn't consider them very religious. Eileen went to Catholic school through high school. *"But I stopped going to church on Sunday when I was about fifteen because I couldn't buy into the fear and guilt anymore. It wasn't giving me what I needed."*

Eileen was the youngest of five daughters. Over twelve years separated her from her three oldest sisters, so she was close only to the sister who was four years older.

Eileen now sees the dysfunction in her family that she didn't see while growing up. Her father had a drinking problem, and Eileen and her sisters have all had drinking problems. She said that her parents supplied the basic material needs of a family, but not the emotional needs. Eileen was closer to her father than her mother, but he died when she was eighteen.

At eighteen, Eileen also realized she was gay when she fell in love with another woman. *"I had crushes on women teachers when I was growing up, but I never thought about being gay. All my sisters know, and even though I never told my parents, I think they knew."*

After high school, Eileen worked in New York City for several years and then moved to California to be near the one sister to whom she felt close. She found a customer service job that she has been working in for twenty years.

Eileen's involvement in metaphysics grew first out of a desire to forgive herself for something she had done to a friend. Two years later, she broke up with her lover, and her sister moved out of state. *"Everyone was leaving me, and I felt a great sense of loss. Then I saw Shirley MacLaine talking about her Higher Self seminars on a talk show. I didn't know what I was getting into, but I felt I had to call right away to register for one the next month. I thought it would help me forgive myself."*

Eileen said it helped her do that and much more. *"I had never meditated before and didn't know what to expect, but I got into it easily. I contacted my higher self, and I soared. It's something I'll never forget. Since then my life has turned around, and I'm seeing the world with such different eyes now because my consciousness has changed."*

After sharing that weekend with five hundred people, Eileen felt lost when she got home and didn't know who to turn to for support to continue the work she had started. She found a local metaphysical magazine and looked for groups she could get involved with. *"I came across an ad for a metaphysical center that had meditation and Sunday services. I decided to go, which was way out of character for me. I wasn't the type to go to new places on my own, and I hadn't been in a church in years. But I found a niche there and have been going every week. Everyone there understands where I'm coming from."*

Eileen began meditating every day to build up a power within herself. But when she came home from work feeling stressed, she would drink a few beers to relax. *"I felt I was negating what I was building through meditation. When you get into metaphysics, the name of the game is getting control over your life. I wrote an affirmation in January saying I would stop drinking by March. A week later, I stopped. I quit smoking two years earlier using the same higher power."*

Eileen says she appreciates much more of life now, especially nature. She enjoys watching birds in her back yard and has started gardening.

She also spends time in self-observation, especially at work. *"I've been practicing it for six months. Sometimes I can step out of myself and observe myself. I can catch when I'm using a negative tone of voice, and I can change it.*"

Eileen is taking a class at the spiritual center that requires reading several esoteric, spiritual books. *"The center doesn't have a particular philosophy that it teaches. They make a lot of ideas available, but they encourage us not to believe anything that we can't prove to ourselves or that doesn't feel comfortable."*

Every month Eileen tries to do something new. *"Here I am 45 years old, and I went to the movies by myself for the first time four months ago. I'm removing my limits and blocks one at a time. I always liked myself, but now I love myself. And I love being by myself."*

But she also spends more time with people. Having more friendships was another of the affirmations she wrote in January. *"I'm not working at it, it just happens. I find that writing down affirmations makes them more likely to happen. Last year, I wrote that I wanted to lose thirty pounds. I lost the thirty pounds, but didn't lose anymore even though I followed the same routine. And my weight has stayed the same since."*

Eileen is considering changing her job after twenty years because she is tired of the pressure of dealing with angry customers and personnel turnover. *"I use breathing techniques to settle or calm myself, and I let go of the stress from work as soon as I walk in my door at home."*

Life Goals

For now, Eileen prefers to just let things happen rather than plan a specific future. Although she would like to have a relationship again, she said she'd rather concentrate on several other things she wants to do for herself first.

Spiritual Beliefs

Eileen said God is something she feels within her that is more powerful than she is. She feels that God is the only One who knows why we are here. And she is thankful for the experience to touch her soul during the Higher Self seminar.

Growth Techniques

Meditation has been one of the most important techniques for Eileen. *"I do meditation to turn my brain off. When I first started, I practiced forty-five minutes every day using the technique that Shirley MacLaine taught. After practicing for five months, during one mediation a wave of energy went through me. I was aware of white light, and then my mind went blank. Now I can go into that state every time I meditate."*

Eileen also goes to a support group on longevity every two weeks. *"We go over mental, physical, emotional, and spiritual techniques to keep balanced. I think balance is the secret to long life."* Eileen also benefits from the spiritual center she attends and from her love of reading.

Amanda (55, Nazarene background, yoga teacher)

Amanda is just now remembering childhood abuse by her father. She said she sleepwalked through her life until age thirty-eight when her sixteen year old son died. His death broke down the walls that had held back her assertiveness and strength. She divorced, then considered suicide, but made it through the first year on her own. Her nearly twenty years of recovery include learning about yoga and nutrition, healing her inner child, living for several months in a spiritual community, and traveling to India.

Life Story

Amanda's mother had a Christian Science background, but she and Amanda went to the Nazarene church. The fact that her mother went to church but her father didn't gave Amanda mixed signals as to its importance. As an adult, she long felt that her religious background had not served her well. Now she concedes that having a strong religious background helped keep her focused on spiritual growth even though her direction has changed.

Amanda said she was a "mousy, passive woman" before and during her marriage and lived her life through her husband. She sleepwalked through her life until age thirty-eight when the death of her youngest son at sixteen shattered that sleep. *"I was concerned when he didn't come home from a walk. I heard a siren, but I thought it went on into town so I didn't go out to check. When the police came to the door, I knew instantly that he was dead."*

At the funeral home, she argued with the funeral director to see her son and surprised herself with her assertiveness. She took charge of everything, leaving her husband free to succumb to his grief.

The next night, while her husband slept, Amanda felt her son's "presence" walk into their bedroom and stand beside her. She was frightened and said to him, *"I don't know why I'm afraid, but I am."* Her son paused for a moment and left. Amanda immediately regretted expressing her fear instead of her love to him. But she was comforted to discover there was another world that she hadn't known anything about.

She remembered that her son had introduced her to the concept of reincarnation. *"He used to play for hours with army toys. At fourteen, he told me he thought he had been in Napoleon's army."*

His death made Amanda look closely at her own life. She didn't want to continue living a life doing the same things without making any progress. She thought about leaving her husband years before, but didn't have the courage. She had started psychotherapy nine years before which helped her to stay in the marriage, but never seemed to get at the core of her problems. At thirty-eight, she started to think about her escape so that she could start to heal.

A few years later, Amanda's husband became close with a woman colleague. One day when Amanda's daughter announced she liked her daddy more than her mother, Amanda saw a way out. She and her husband decided to divorce and their daughter would live with her father. *"Leaving them was the hardest thing I've done in my life. I knew that if I left, my husband would remarry. He did within a year, so my daughter had another mother."*

After the divorce, Amanda started to read books about suicide and near-death experiences. *"I attempted suicide about six years before my son died. I learned it was harder than I thought, and I vowed there would never be another 'attempt.' I would either not try or make sure it was successful."* Thinking about suicide became an obsession, but she made it through that first year on her own.

Then Amanda took an office job. Within a year, she took in her mother who had inoperable cancer. She eventually moved her mother into a Christian Science nursing home where she spent her last few months. One night, Amanda had a dream about her mother running toward her with great effort. She awoke and wanted to check on her mother, but her lack of assertiveness returned, and she decided not to disturb the nurses in the middle of the night. And her mother died that night. *"I had an unfinished feeling about that, but I also had evidence that I could know things in a different way."*

While married, Amanda had become overweight, had chronic health problems, and was in the doctor's office at least once a month. As part of her new life, she investigated holistic health, changed her diet, took vitamins, stopped going to doctors, and said she started to feel better.

Her oldest son recommended a workshop called Actualizations, developed by one of Werner Erhard's trainers in the est[7] program. She said that workshop changed her perception of the world.

---

7. est is an abbreviation for Erhard Seminars Training, personal growth seminars that became popular in the late 1970's.

Next, she investigated spiritual communities, chose one, and visited it for a month. *"One morning at the end of the month, I felt very clearly that if I just 'let go,' I could leave the earth and go to another dimension. But three things ran through my mind that held me back. I hadn't been out for my morning run. I hadn't had breakfast. And I couldn't leave my family without saying good-bye. So I stayed."*

Amanda went home and sold all her belongings so she could go back to the community for an extended period. She returned to it and practiced yoga, breath work, meditation, and studied different philosophies.

After a few months, she had an experience that the others in the community couldn't handle. *"I shifted into another energy place that was totally different from where I had been. I had so much energy that I hardly slept. I was happy and wrote poetry. One night I left my body and seemed to tumble in space feeling great pleasure. When I got tired or felt afraid, I could come right back to my body."*

Because of the changes in her behavior, the people in the community took her to a mental hospital. She said she knew that wasn't what she needed, but her companions insisted. *"It was hard to live there because I was used to silence and the staff played loud music. I was used to a pure atmosphere, but the nurse's smoke would wake me up. I refused all the drugs because I had a problem getting off prescription drugs before and didn't want to go through that again."*

After she left the hospital, the urge to continue her spiritual growth returned, and she traveled to India with some friends, staying on by herself after they returned home. She hadn't traveled much before and never out of the country. She credits that trip with giving her the opportunity to break old patterns.

When Amanda returned, she took one office job after another, but realized she had a problem making a transition back into society. *"I promised myself then that I was not going to work at a job where I suffered. I told myself I didn't have to succeed in anything. All I had to do with my life was stick it out and do whatever makes me feel better about it."* She wanted to work at something that expressed who she was. The two things she loved to do were yoga and gardening. She didn't make much money raising and selling vegetables, so she focused on teaching yoga.

As her body loosened up from practicing and teaching yoga, repressed memories of childhood abuse surfaced, and she realized they were the core issues that needed healing.

At first, Amanda felt upset, hurt, and angry with her father and wanted to avoid dealing with the memories. Then she acknowledged the problem, but wanted to heal it as fast as possible to get on with her life.

Finally, she realized that the pain and healing was as much a part of her life as anything else and deserved her full attention.

Amanda understands now that her father just followed the same pattern from his childhood. Amanda admits that she unwittingly passed it along by severely spanking her son until reading an article helped her realize her displaced emotions. *"Although my 'protective self' won't allow actual memories of the incest, I feel it happened only once when he was drunk. He quit drinking when I was about five and stopped the beatings soon after that."* The changes he made in his life without any of the tools available today amazes her. *"I think the giant step he made may have helped me to make changes in my own life. And I think there was more love there than I knew."*

Amanda recently quit a part-time job that supplemented her yoga teaching income. She said it was the first time she had made such a change without creating trouble around it, which she calls progress. *"Even though my financial situation is scary, I have to trust that everything will be taken care of if I do what feels right."*

Amanda tries to go to the mountains as often as possible to refresh her spirit. Since every day seems like a holiday, she has no desire to escape her daily life.

Spiritual Beliefs

Amanda tries to sit quietly once a day, connecting to her deepest self. She uses techniques to clear herself of negative energy and to put a protective force around herself. Her highest priority is to continue her own healing process.

Amanda sees God as the "Source" to which her essence is connected rather than being separate from her.

Growth Techniques

Amanda finds the most difficulty in resisting the pull of the past and supporting herself financially.

Louise Hay's books and *The Power of the Spoken Word* by Florence Scovel Shinn helped Amanda realize how important words and thoughts are in creating her life. She noticed that part of her mind wants to rant and rave about "bad things." She calls that the "anti-life" force and finds joy when she can acknowledge it without letting it control her.

As part of her healing, Amanda decided to have a massage by a male therapist to experience a masculine touch that felt nurturing and safe. She said the more she lets go of decisions she made about the world as a child, the more gentle and flowing her healing process is.

Some of the other resources she has used to deal with the abuse are rebirthing[8,] group therapy, Terry Kellogg's videos and Ellen Bass and Laura Davis's book, *The Courage to Heal*. When she feels a money pinch, she trades her books or tapes with others.

The Future

Amanda doesn't see a holocaust in the planet's future. Although she concedes that many people generate negative thoughts, she sees many others putting out positive and healing thoughts.

She sees more people becoming aware of energy and feels that "waves of healing" are forming on the planet. She thinks the change in energy will cause societal and political changes. *"People who don't want change will have the most problems. It's like a dawn and a lot of people are waking up. Eventually, as it gets lighter and lighter, everybody will wake up."*

Roené (36, Anglican background, free-lance sales)

Catholic school turned Roené away from religion for many years. A series of painful relationships and a marriage that stole her identity led her to seek help from Alcoholics Anonymous, a rebirther[9], and Avatar training. She is developing a new identity that brings her happiness, peace, and the hope of loving relationships.

Life Story

As a child, Roené was comforted by her awareness of God in nature and other people. That comfort was destroyed after she began attending an Anglican church in Canada that portrayed God as punishing and watching for her to make mistakes. When she was ten, Roené's family moved to the United States, and she was sent to a Catholic girls' school. *"I hated the limiting and guilt-ridden religion I found there. I blocked my fear that God wanted to punish me. I used to think, 'Stay out of my life, and I'll stay out of yours.' I avoided religious experiences for years after that."*

---

8. Rebirthing is a technique that focuses on the breath to facilitate emotional release and healing. It was developed by Leonard Orr and is used in Sondra Ray's Loving Relationships Training.

9. A person trained in rebirthing. Rebirthing is a technique that focuses on the breath to facilitate emotional release and healing. It was developed by Leonard Orr and is used in Sondra Ray's Loving Relationships Training.

Roené had an interest in metaphysics, however, and pursued it after high school. She took a course in astrology and did charts for people, considering it as a possible career.

At twenty-three, Roené wanted to go to Europe, particularly England to study astrology. She went to Europe for two years, but wandered away from her metaphysical interests. *"I decided to try to be a normal person. I came home and got a degree in fashion design to please my parents. I did very well in school and went to work in New York. But I quit after three weeks because I didn't enjoy it."* Roené did stay in the fashion field, however, for another five years.

During those years, Roené had a few relationships that always ended with rejection and pain. *"I ran around with deep, dark thoughts that I couldn't have what I wanted, that I was a failure, and that nobody loved me."* Roené continued to read metaphysical books, looking for an explanation for her life. She credits Vernon Howard's book, *Mystic Path to Cosmic Power,* with giving her some important insights.

At twenty-nine, Roené's discouragement led her to believe she would never get married or have what she wanted. A year later, however, she entered "a miserable marriage" that lasted three and a half years. *"I lost my identity trying to please my husband. His interests were eating, sleeping, working, and sunbathing. He was boring."* He didn't want children and asked Roené to have surgery to be sure she couldn't, but she wouldn't agree to it. He also insisted on separate bank accounts for his protection. *"Every time I tried to appease him, a new conflict would arise and the more critical he was."*

As a last resort, Roené went to a psychic for advice to save her marriage. The psychic told her to buy *The Dynamic Laws of Prosperity,* a book by Catherine Ponder. Before she could read the book, Roené discovered her husband's girlfriends, and he presented divorce papers. *"I felt totally lost by that time. But Catherine Ponder's book said that God is not a punishing God and would provide me with whatever I needed."* Roené read the book every day, practicing its principles of prayer and forgiveness. She was happy to find that the divorce went smoother than she imagined.

Three days after her divorce, on Easter Sunday, Roené went to the Unity church with some girlfriends. She felt comfortable there because no one told her what to believe or encouraged guilt. She could be herself, with no rules. She sought counseling and entered into another relationship which resulted in her being hurt again.

A Unity friend suggested Roené try rebirthing to release her emotional traumas. *"While I was waiting for my rebirthing appointment, I went to a bookstore for a book on life after divorce and instead bought two books by Sondra Ray, Loving Relationships and I Deserve Love. I took the Loving*

Relationships Training and started reading all the books I could by Sondra Ray and Leonard Orr."

Other books that were important to her were the five volume series *Life and Teaching of the Masters of the Far East* by Baird T. Spalding, *Women Who Love Too Much* by Robin Norwood, and *Men Who Hate Women & the Women Who Love Them* by Susan Forward and Joan Torres. *"Those books helped me shift out of my victim/martyr consciousness."*

As an adult child of an alcoholic, Roené found support at Alcoholics Anonymous. *"They started me thinking that I could control my life. I started to believe that I didn't have to be a failure."*

In late 1987, she discovered Avatar training, a personal growth program developed by Harry Palmer. *"The program taught me how to create the reality I wanted and how to always be happy. I learned to control my reactions to life experiences. I see my beliefs creating my experiences rather than the reverse."*

Her spiritual growth has taken top priority in her life. She recently let go of many of the negative beliefs she had about men and relationships. She has noticed more men flirting with her and feels relaxed and comfortable with it. She looks forward to creating the relationship she wants and feels she deserves.

Life Goals

Roené has a part-time sales job but plans for a full-time career running a local Avatar training center. Now that she feels so good about herself, she wants to help others on their journey.

Spiritual Beliefs

Roené says that everything is secondary to her spiritual self. She loves God absolutely and describes Him as a beautiful, radiant being who shares what He has with everyone. She says we all have the same powers as He has; we just need to recognize and awaken the God-self within.

"I have wonderful gifts called 'free will' and 'creation' that I can call on at any time." Roené called guilt a man-made creation and rejects it in order to avoid separation, suffering, and sacrifice. She says we are all creators and create from our beliefs. She can change her belief or opinion about a person or situation and experience it differently. She knows nothing can take her joy away.

She called prosperity a gift that people can accept or reject out of guilt or a belief that they must suffer or don't deserve it. In order to live fully and happily, she said one must be prosperous. *"One's attitude towards prosperity must be kept in balance-you can't let 'things' be more important than you are. On the other hand, you shouldn't starve your mind, body, or soul out of guilt or sacrifice. Prosperity and spirituality are the same and we all deserve it."*

The purpose of life, according to Roené, is for spirit to take on a physical body and its limits as part of the process of learning that everyone is a creator. She sees life's obstacles as lessons that she creates and knows she can choose to learn from and move past them. She looks forward to challenges because she knows they stimulate growth. *"As each person heals and grows, he has a greater energy that attracts others. The more people heal individually, the healthier the world as a whole will be."*

Growth Techniques

Meditation and rebirthing have served Roené as tools for releasing emotional trauma. She looks for the emotional and mental reasons behind health problems to identify her lessons. Books, Alcoholics Anonymous, and the Avatar training have been important catalysts for her growth. Finally, Roené says that a network of fellow seekers provides support and a safe environment for her own journey.

Gail (43, Lutheran background, residential counselor)

Gail was sexually abused by her father, abused by an alcoholic step-father, and finally separated from her brother when her mother died. While in an unhappy marriage, she had a mystical experience that explained the reasons for all the unhappiness she had experienced. Withthe help of talk and body-oriented psychotherapies, Gail has finally stabilized her life and enjoys her job working with the mentally ill.

Life Story

Gail was sexually molested by her father when she was eight months old, and her parents divorced when she was three. Then Gail, her mother, and brother lived with her grandmother for a few years.

When Gail was eight, her mother remarried. *"My step-father was an alcoholic, nice when sober but violent when drunk. My brother and I lived in constant fear for almost four years."*

When Gail was eleven, her mother died, which resulted in Gail and her brother being separated. Gail alternated living with an uncle and her grandmother, while her brother lived with another uncle.

Gail went to the Lutheran church every Sunday, but it never answered questions for her. It didn't fill the emptiness she felt inside. *"We said a prayer at meals, but we didn't discuss theology at home. Everyone accepted what the ministers said. But I had questions about contradictions I saw in the teachings, and there was no one in the family I could talk to about them."*

Gail's father visited a few years after her mother died. *"Everyone had told me horrible things about him. When he came to visit, I hid in the basement and shook in fear. There was a part of me that wanted to go up and see what he looked like, a part that remembered and loved him. But the part that was afraid was stronger."*

Gail said her teenage years were fairly normal. She was involved in sports, cheerleading, dated, drank, and smoke. But she also read avidly, especially about psychic phenomena and science fiction. *"I also read a trashy romance that opened my eyes about people. The story portrayed a prostitute's life and explained what she went through as a child and why she ended up the way she did. I realized you couldn't judge somebody by who they are now. You have to look at what brought them to where they are."* But there was no one with whom Gail could discuss her interests and insights about people. *"When I talked to my friends about it, they thought I was kooky, but interesting."*

Gail also had a problem because she developed physically earlier than her friends. *"The guys whistled, and the girls were jealous. But inside I thought my body was dirty, and I never felt comfortable with it."*

After high school, Gail moved to another city and got a job. *"Then I married out of a need for security and a father figure. After the sexual excitement wore off, I realized that my husband and I had different interests. He was stable and dependable, but I couldn't discuss my thoughts and spiritual matters with him."*

When Gail was twenty-one, her father was dying in a veteran's hospital. *"I visited him and realized he wasn't the ogre my relatives had painted him to be. He tried to explain the difficult times in his life and to make amends to me. That really opened me up to seeing someone else's side of the story. I felt the loss of never knowing what having a father was and never knowing what security was. At his funeral, I was sad that I had no feelings for him."*

Not long after, Gail had an affair and fell in love. *"I felt a connection of our spirits, and I enjoyed talking to him in a way that I couldn't with my husband. But our guilt was too strong for it to last."*

That breakup triggered a depression in Gail. *"One day while lying in bed, I said, 'I wish there were a God.' Something in me gave up then."*

Later that day, Gail walked into the living room and collapsed on the floor. *"I must have been there for four hours. I became one with everything. I had no control, and I didn't care. I became part of the sky. I knew what clouds felt like, what trees felt like. I was happy to be dirt. I appreciated the nurturing essence of it. I had a feeling of 'I am.' I was a part of all those things. Suddenly,*

I saw why my life had been the way it was. Everything had worked for me to have this experience. The pain in my life. The books I had read. The words 'seek and ye shall find' and 'knock and the door shall be opened' came to me. I finally knew what they meant."

"Near the end of the experience, I felt compassion and understanding of what Jesus really came for. He didn't come to be worshipped, but to teach that we could all have the knowledge he has. I recognized his tremendous love and compassion, and I tried to explain the experience to other people so they would know what I had learned. Now I realize that was futile; people have to have their own experiences."

Gail called the experience a blessing and a curse. She said her ego wasn't ready to handle it. She knew she had a purpose that would help other people, but she hadn't worked emotionally on her own wounds. In the next several months, she smoked marijuana and took LSD in an attempt to continue the spiritual experience. *"Everything was coming in so fast. I appreciated everything and was full of love. But it was more than I was ready for. I started feeling paranoid and having delusions and then manic-depressive episodes."*

In desperate need for stability, Gail reconciled with her estranged husband. She had two more manic-depressive episodes, each time she had been trying to break up with her husband, which triggered her issues over loss. *"My husband was very logical. When I tried to talk to him about my feelings, he would say, 'That's stupid.' And he would tell me what I needed to do logically. So there was no validation of my feelings. What I really needed was the release of my feelings."*

After her last manic-depressive episode, Gail decided to see a psychiatrist. *"He was excellent. He was Jungian, spiritual, nurturing, and got me into my feelings. For the first three years of therapy, I cried for all the losses, misunderstandings, pain, and confusion."*

After the first six months of therapy, Gail started taking college psychology courses. Then she learned about meditation and relaxation techniques. *"I was amazed at how well I did in school. I found something on which to focus my energy."* After graduation, Gail and her husband separated and Gail went to work in a center for the chronically mentally ill. She sees her own experiences contributing to her ability to work so well with her clients.

Gail went home to see her family two years before the interview for this book and was hurt that no one asked her what she did. *"I don't know if they weren't interested or they just didn't know how to relate to me. I know I'm not going to get the understanding from them that I get from friends who share the journey."* She feels a particular sense of loss about her brother. *"I was very protective of him growing up. Now he thinks my life is kooky. And he's a workaholic.*"

But Gail does have a support group she can count on to help her balance her spiritual and emotional sides. And now she's working on physical issues. *"I've decided I don't need my extra weight as a defense anymore.*" She and some friends are losing weight through Weight Watchers. The book, *On the Way to the Wedding* by Linda S. Leonard, helped her realize why she was eating so much. *"I ate to push down fear, anxiety, and anger. And it took away my femininity and creative energies.*"

Life Goals

Gail said she was ready for a job change and was interested in training in bioenergetics[10] She was also ready for a relationship after five years without one. *"I would like someone to share the journey with. It's scary and exciting, and I look forward to the physical nurturing since I'm more in touch with my body.*"

Spiritual Beliefs

Gail sees everything as part of a whole. *"The air between all of us has an energy of its own, and it connects us. If we could just accept our connection to everything else, we would be joyful.*"

Gail said that struggles in her life bring her lessons. *"I don't believe the world is going to blow up and end. I believe the situation is serious, but we need to see problems as lessons. We need to apply what we learn to our communities. I can look at ugly things that happen and see the good that comes from them, and I can appreciate it and thank it.*"

Growth Techniques

Gail said her interests are more in psychological and spiritual areas than in psychic phenomena. Gail has benefitted from guided imagery, creative visualization, and meditation.

Gail has used bioenergetics as a tool to release fears and unresolved emotions. *"I love the intense work. In a weekend, you can see people discovering and clearing things that may take four or five years of talk therapy.*"

Gail has also been an avid reader. Ken Wilber is one of her favorite authors, and she worked with *A Course in Miracles*[11] for two years.

---

10. Bioenergetics is a form of body-oriented psychotherapy which uses movement and breathing exercises to open up muscular-emotional blocks.

11. *A Course in Miracles* is a three part set of books that was channeled by an unidentified voice (belived to be Christ) to an atheistic research psychologist over a seven year period starting in 1965. The books consist of a Textbook, a Workbook for Students consisting of 365 daily lessons, and a Manual for Teachers.

Update (March 1990)

Gail had changed jobs and said she loves her new job facilitating groups in a program for the long-term mentally ill.

Greg (55, Baptist background, in transition)

Emotional abuse from his adoptive mother led Greg to alcohol abuse. His alcoholism ruined his first marriage and led him to attempt suicide. With the help of Alcoholics Anonymous and a few other spiritual people who came into his life, Greg has stopped drinking and now has a successful relationship and plans for a new career.

Life Story

Greg was adopted when he was nine months old. His adoptive brother and sister were several years older, so he essentially grew up as an only child, except that his mother continually compared him unfavorably to his older brother. *"My first report card in first grade had perfect ratings and a comment that I tended to talk too much. I was excited until my mother focused only on the comment and said that my brother would never have had a comment like that on his report card. That was all she said about it."*

Greg grew up in a small town in Tennessee and was baptized in the Baptist church when he was twelve. *"I was pushed into it. At age sixteen, I started asking questions about the Bible, especially the contradictions in it. When the pastor called me in to tell me I was a troublemaker, I dropped out of the church."*

Being compared to his older brother went on throughout Greg's childhood and teen years. *"I always came up short. I had a strong sense of failure, no self-confidence, and little self-worth. There are many parts of my childhood I have blocked from my memory because they were so painful."*

Greg's father tried to act as a buffer between Greg and his mother, but he wasn't very effective. Greg attributes that to the poor relationship he saw between his mother and father. *"My father was the only one I had any good feelings about. He was an alcoholic but had stopped drinking before I was born."* Greg never brought friends home because his mother always criticized them as not being good enough for him.

Greg started drinking about age twelve when his brother came home after World War II. *"By the time I was twenty and in the service, I was a full-fledged alcoholic-drunk every day. I didn't believe anyone could love me because*

I was no good. But the booze allowed me to cut that tape off. I could live in a fantasy world and be anything I wanted to be."

After the service, Greg went to college for a science degree and married in his sophomore year. *"I did a lot of controlled drinking during college so that my wife didn't know I had a problem. After graduation, I got a job as an engineer. Once I had more money to spend, I started drinking again on a regular basis."*

After a three-day blackout, Greg followed his doctor's recommendation to go to Alcoholics Anonymous. But Greg felt it was too late for his marriage. *"My wife harbored too many resentments. She told me she had put up with seven years of crap from me and was going to get in her seven years."*

Greg's life began to change after he started going to AA. His wife wouldn't go to Alcoholics Anonymous because she thought the problem was all his. *"She didn't realize the effect on her of living with an alcoholic for all those years. We had two or three good years together after I went into AA. But then our relationship deteriorated because I was changing at a pretty rapid rate and she wasn't changing at all. I think she was jealous of AA. From her point of view, I hadn't been willing to get sober for her and the kids, but I did it for a bunch of strangers."*

Learning to turn his life over to a higher power as AA suggests, Greg's spiritual search began. *"I tried to go to a moderate Christian church, but I was still uncomfortable with the concept of dualism."*

But more problems were ahead for Greg. He became so fed up with what he saw as incompetency and politics in his company that he walked out on his job one day and never went back. Instead, he went to work on the waterfront where he could leave his worries about work behind the minute he left the dock. During the five years he worked there, Greg's brother and mother died. Greg eventually resorted to selling marijuana and amphetamines to make enough money to settle with his wife so he could end his marriage.

But Greg was arrested when he tried to make a sale to an undercover police officer. *"They were sentencing people to forty years for those crimes. My lawyer had the trial postponed for two years, and I hung in limbo. I pleaded guilty to the sales charges and the other charges were reduced."*

"Before the sentencing, a new friend, who was a recovered alcoholic and into New Age thought, told me I would be free. At the sentencing the judge called my attorney into his office. When my attorney came out, he said, 'I don't know if you believe in God, but something is about to happen in this courtroom that I haven't seen in thirty years of practicing law. You're getting unsupervised probation. You're totally free.' Having expected a long prison sentence, this outcome told me there was a reason for me to be free. I intensified my search to

find out what I was supposed to be doing in this life. I knew I was free because the universe had a plan for me that didn't include twenty years in prison."

Greg started dating another friend who was also a recovered alcoholic and interested in New Age thought. She introduced him to books on Eastern religions, psychic phenomena, and channeling. *"At first, I thought that stuff was just garbage. But strange things began to happen. I had conscious out-of-body experiences, and I had a past-life reading that explained several things that had happened to me that I had no other explanation for. So for me, the concept of reincarnation answered a lot of questions."*

When Greg broke up with his girlfriend a couple of years later, he started drinking again after twelve years of being sober. *"After drinking for two months, one night I drank a fifth of whiskey between six and eleven p.m. and concluded that life wasn't worth living anymore. So I got out my gun, loaded it, and put it to my temple. When I told myself, 'Pull the trigger,' I couldn't feel anything from my shoulder to my hand. I couldn't feel my fingers or the gun. I lowered it, pointed it at the wall, and pulled the trigger, blowing a hole in the wall. I put it back to my head and again nothing happened. I blew eleven holes in my bedroom wall that night trying to blow my brains out. But I couldn't feel my hand or the gun when it was pointed at my head. I finally ended up saying, 'God, I don't know if you exist. But if you do, I can't live, and I can't die. If you exist, show me how to live.'"*

Greg got an answer one morning two weeks later. *"I was reading in bed when the room got intensely bright. I felt a sense of joy, peace, and bliss that no words can describe. Tears rolled down my face. I think it lasted about ten or twenty minutes. Slowly, the room returned to normal. That proved to me the existence of something greater than myself. I began searching to understand what I had experienced that morning. It happened again about a month later, although not as intensely. I walked away from the waterfront and never went back because I knew I couldn't stay sober there. I've been sober ever since."*

And that experience prompted Greg to renew his spiritual search. He looked for answers to the questions, "Who am I?" "Where am I going?" and "Why am I here?" And he had more out-of-body and psychic experiences that made him more passionate about his search.

Gradually, Greg reentered the world he had turned his back on almost five years before. He went back to work in a management position and learned to make decisions without condemning himself later if they turned out to be wrong. Instead, he looked at mistakes as a learning experience. He discovered that even the act of firing or disciplining an employee could be done with love.

By the time of the interview, Greg had been in a satisfying relationship for over five years. Six months before the interview, his company shut down leaving him time for his first vacation in five years. He was taking several months off as a sabbatical and to investigate starting a new business.

Spiritual Beliefs

Greg believes in the concepts of reincarnation and karma. He sees each lifetime as an opportunity to evolve spiritually on a journey back to "the One or God." He is careful about his actions because he believes anything he does has an effect on every living thing on the planet at some level. But he doesn't believe in judging something as "good" or "bad." Instead, "it just is." When something people consider "bad" happens, he is satisfied that it is in harmony with God's overall plan which only He knows.

"Several years ago, all I could see were the differences in religious philosophies. Now I am beginning to see the sameness in religions. If you dig deep enough, the core philosophy is essentially identical among them. In Buddhism, it is compassion for every living thing. In Christianity, it is love. Now I see the universality of all religions."

Greg said that the major change in himself due to his spiritual search is that now he loves himself. *"I'm no longer a failure, an unworthy human being loaded with resentments, envious of other people. Most of the people I had resentments against I have forgiven and let go. In fact, I opened communications with my sister two years ago for the first time in seven years. She said I was a different person. I learned that I could turn my life around as soon as I became willing to let it happen."* Greg cited several examples of rewarding jobs that came his way once he dropped his ego and self-centeredness and became willing to do any honest work.

Through experience, Greg has learned that his thoughts bring what comes to him. *"If I am afraid of failure or financial insecurity, those things are going to happen."* His attitude toward material things now is to appreciate them but not to let them own him by being so attached to them that he worries about losing them.

Greg believes that part of his lesson in this life was to overcome alcoholism. *"I know I have had several lifetimes as an alcoholic and didn't overcome it. And there are some karmic debts between my older son and me that have to be worked out. I think this incarnation is one of the most growth-oriented ones I have been through in a long time."*

In advising others who are dissatisfied with their current spiritual teachings, Greg advises they look at new things and keep an open mind. *"If you hear something that seems to make sense to you and you incorporate it into your life and it enhances the quality of your life, then use it. If it creates chaos or emotional turmoil, it isn't a truth for you regardless of what anyone else says.*

Don't get upset about it; stick it on the shelf. It may turn into a truth for you ten years down the road. Have the strength to say, 'Hey, that's not for me,' and keep looking for what is right for you."

Kris (33, no religious background, in transition)

Kris decided very early that marriage and a family were not for her. She wasn't going to let herself get involved in a relationship like those she saw growing up. In her first year after college, she faced a career and health crisis. She used rebirthing, Louise Hay's books and her own intuition to overcome those crises, leaving her more at peace than she has ever felt.

Life Story

Although her heritage is Jewish, Kris's family was not very involved in the religion, and Kris didn't pursue it on her own.

From an early age, Kris realized how much her mother loved her father and that her father didn't return that love. *"When I was about five, I asked my dad if he had the choice to do it all over again, would he. He said, 'I don't know.' I wish he would have lied."*

Kris said she took on the role of mediator in the house to help relieve the tension. She also noticed that most of her parents' friends had relationship problems. *"By the time I was a teenager, I had decided I never wanted to get married or have kids. I had never seen an example of a relationship that I would want to be involved in. So I figured I would be independent, spend time with people when I wanted to, and then move on."*

Kris remembered laughing often until she was fifteen. She doesn't recall what caused the laughter to stop, but she became very serious. *"I remember wondering how the other kids on the school bus could laugh with a war (Vietnam) on."*

About that time, Kris fell in love for the first time. *"After we made love, my boyfriend said he couldn't respect me. When he left, I considered suicide. That left an emotional scar that I am still trying to heal."*

Kris was always a good student. She only took a week off between high school and college and between undergraduate and graduate school. And working as a secretary while going to college left her little time for a social life.

After graduate school, Kris moved from New York to Los Angeles. That first year starting a new career in a new city was a nightmare for Kris. *"Until that time, I had always been able to create what I wanted in my life. When I got to California, I suddenly felt disconnected from my source. I felt I had forgotten everything I had ever known about myself. I think the problem was that I was afraid and my fear blocked my faith."*

Kris had problems at work and felt as if she had forgotten everything she had learned in school. But she also feels that was an important learning experience for her. *"Coming from New York, I had no tolerance for people who were incompetent or indecisive. By experiencing it myself, I was able to give up my judgments about other people."*

Kris became very ill during that year, and traditional medicine wasn't able to help her, so she took responsibility for healing herself. She used megavitamin therapy and Silva Mind Control to work on her physical symptoms. *"Eventually, I was led to look at the emotional level. Louise Hay's book (You Can Heal Your Life) about emotional and mental causes of illness became my bible. I realized how cut off I was from my emotions. So that first year was an opportunity to discover myself in a much deeper way."*

Kris said that her nature is to make changes. When she feels it is time for a change, she just does it. *"I don't follow a logical decision process. My mind can't conceive of the next steps for me. Things just happen."*

When she started rebirthing[12] on her thirtieth birthday, Kris said that was the beginning of her life opening up and changing. For a while when she was going through some changes, Kris wanted her family to change too. *"I was very evangelistic about it, which was probably nauseating for them. Then when I finally did let go of my attachment to their changing, my parents thought I didn't need them anymore."*

Kris began to sense that her time in Los Angeles was ending. *"I woke up one day and felt that it was time to leave, not only the city but my profession. So I resigned and went on vacation."*

Kris was worried about money and what new career she would pursue, but after a while, she became comfortable with her concern. *"One night before bed, I said, 'I'm ready to know where I'm to go.' A few months before, I had said I wanted to live in a place near woods, mountains, and the ocean. I wanted a small town environment with a high social consciousness and access to organically grown foods. When I finished with those requirements, I laughed to myself thinking there was no such place in the world. When I woke up the next morning, I blurted out the name of a town I had never heard of. I visited a friend in San Francisco and discovered the town was near there. When I drove to it, I saw a sign for the mountains, woods, and beach."*

---

12. Rebirthing. Rebirthing is a technique that focuses on the breath to facilitate emotional release and healing. It was developed by Leonard Orr and is used in Sondra Ray's Loving Relationships Training.

Immediately, Kris packed and moved there. *"People thought I was brave to drop everything and move. But nothing was easier than that move because I knew it was the only right choice for me. When things are easy, I know I'm on the path."*

Kris spent the first few months hiking in the mountains, enjoying nature and the time alone. After a few weeks, she said she started hearing messages from the trees, and most of the messages were about the "art of being." Kris understands "being" as having a connection to the source and allowing it to flow through into the world. She considers the trees as bridges between heaven and earth and feels that people are here to be the same.

Kris said that when she was caught up in her fears, she couldn't hear anything. Communication is clearest for her when she doesn't demand anything and is in the moment, not thinking of the past or future. *"One day when I was hiking and in awe of the paradise of the woods, I suddenly got the message, 'That's all you need to do. You don't have to be in action, you just have to receive me. By receiving me, you nourish me.' Then I realized that's what people want too."*

A few months before the interview, Kris fell in love for the first time as an adult. And this time she is sticking around to work on her issues as they come up. *"My boyfriend has helped me see my dark side the last few weeks, and I'm happy about it. Knowing about it helps to free all the energy I have been using to hide it from myself."*

Life Goals

At the time of the interview, Kris was investigating new career options and was particularly interested in one that would help transform traditional medicine. Whatever happens, she said she never wanted to work just for the money again.

Kris was struggling, however, over taking an active role in creating her life versus waiting for God's Will for her to be revealed. *"I know that whatever I see in my mind will happen. Then I wonder if I am interfering with what is the best path for me. I have to trust that what comes to my mind and feels right is going to be the right path for me. I don't give the future a lot of thought because once I'm in my head, I've lost my connection. If that happens, I fall back on what I've learned about the art of being. When I'm connected, I don't have to worry about anything because I just know how to be."*

Spiritual Beliefs

Kris considers our physical existence a gift and training ground to help us find our connection to the Source or God. *"By recognizing the light in others, I begin to recognize it in myself. I don't look at people as strangers. To me, they're family I haven't met yet. When I can receive myself, I can receive others."*

Growth Techniques

Kris hasn't read many metaphysical books or studied under New Age teachers. She prefers the process of going inside and discovering the universe through her own intuition. She also values the opportunities her relationship has given her to see her flaws and to do something about them.

Rebirthing, Louise Hay, and a form of bodywork called The Basics were important to Kris in taking charge of her physical and emotional health. "Rebirthing helped me to learn to breathe fully again. When I moved to LA, I became a shallow breather because of the smog. Deep breathing can bring up powerful emotions and memories that most people don't want to deal with. Rebirthing also helped me get back in touch with my heart." Kris said that The Basics bodywork also helped her clear old emotions that were trapped in her body.

Leslie (32, Protestant background, actress/waitress)

Leslie grew up with an alcoholic mother and an abusive stepmother. As a teenager, she felt that her life was so out of control that she attempted suicide. After several years of alcohol and drug abuse as an adult, she finally realized that they were the cause of the problems in her life. Alcoholics and Narcotics Anonymous programs helped her regain control of her life and triggered her search for spiritual fulfillment.

Life Story

Leslie said her parents took her brother and her to church because they thought it was something parents should do, not out of any deep religious beliefs of their own. So Leslie and her family switched churches often, going to whichever Protestant church was convenient. *"I don't remember talking about God or spirituality at home. That wasn't part of the real world for my parents."*

Leslie's parents divorced when she was seven, and she lived with her mother, who had a drinking problem. After Leslie's mother threatened her with a knife, Leslie moved in with her father and stepmother.

Leslie said her father didn't drink but was very manipulative. And her stepmother heaped verbal and physical abuse on her from age nine until she left home after high school. *"When I told my dad that my stepmother was hitting me, he told me not to tell anyone because the lawyers would make me live with my mother and she would try to kill me again. Whenever my father tried to stop my stepmother from abusing me, she threatened to take my two half-brothers away from him, and my father would do anything to keep his second family together."*

Leslie said the scars from her stepmother's verbal abuse were more lasting than those from the physical abuse. *"My self-esteem was nonexistent. My stepmother told me I would end up a drunk like my mother. She called me a slut when I was 11, and I didn't even know what it meant. Then she started sending me to psychiatrists."*

Although Leslie's mother had visitation rights, she stopped seeing Leslie when she was twelve. *"I felt so helpless. My mother was gone, and I had no control over what my stepmother was doing to me."* Leslie started doing whatever she could to get out of the house and became a teenage workaholic-baby-sitting and cleaning houses. *"The workaholic behavior helped me avoid dealing with the situation at home and gave me money, which meant power to me. I still have big issues with work, money, and power."*

Leslie was introduced to drugs at fourteen and started dealing them for the money and popularity they brought. When she used drugs, she felt as if she were "Wonder Woman" and that she could do anything. By sixteen, she started drinking. *"I got drunk the first time and drank like an alcoholic from the start. I thought I had found the answer for me-working hard and using drugs and alcohol."*

The only positive outlet Leslie found in high school was theater. People liked her work, but it wasn't enough to overcome the negative parts of her life. *"I tried to kill myself when I was seventeen. I stole pills from houses where I baby-sat. At school one day, I took drugs and alcohol and made a big scene. Another time I got drunk and took a razor blade to my arms. I was so drunk, it was like watching another person do it."*

Leslie moved away from home after high school and got a job in a bank. When she wasn't working, her life revolved around sex and drugs while she waited for the "right man" to come along and "fix" her. *"I had no goals or plans for my life. I stopped acting. I thought the next job, the next apartment, or the next boyfriend would make me happy. When I changed them and they didn't work, I would start over."*

Leslie tried the hotel business for a few years and was successful in her job and in hiding her drinking from her co-workers. She heard from her mother during that time and found that she had started going to Alcoholics Anonymous.

Leslie's drinking finally interfered with her work, and she had to quit. She decided that the problem was her career, so she decided to change it. She found part-time work as a pre-school teacher, drank in the evenings, and went to work with a hangover a couple of days a week.

One afternoon while drinking at home, Leslie saw the movie *Days of Wine and Roses*. *"It was about two alcoholics, one who stops drinking with the help of Alcoholics Anonymous and the other who keeps on drinking and dies. By the end of the movie, I was petrified and in tears. I called my mother, who was shocked to hear from me after all those years. She had married a man in AA and asked me to visit."* One reason Leslie decided to go was just to feel safe because she had recently been raped at knife point in her apartment and lived in terror of it happening again.

Even after moving to her mother's house, Leslie didn't consider alcohol as a cause for her problems. She tried a few AA meetings but didn't think she was an alcoholic. Leslie's mother offered her the opportunity to go back to school, and she accepted. After winning the lead role in plays for three years, she decided on a theater major. *"That's the way things happen for me. I didn't decide that I was going to be an actress. My path gets presented to me, and it's clear what I should be doing if I pay attention."*

Leslie's drinking and drug use were still out of control. She would stop drinking when she was doing a show and then go on a drinking binge when the show closed. She went through detoxification several times, but it never lasted. Leslie tried AA on and off and went to a therapist to deal with issues related to being an adult child of an alcoholic. Meanwhile, Leslie's desire to fulfill her spiritual thirst led her to meditation and the study of pagan practices.

While working on a film, Leslie met a man who was also an alcoholic and used drugs. Leslie became close to him and his friends, who introduced her to heroin. She developed a relationship with one of the men who was ready to kick his habit. When he tried to kick it himself, he nearly died. Leslie finally accepted that they needed help, and they both went to a Narcotics Anonymous meeting and then entered a treatment program. *"In a way, I'm glad I used heroin instead of drinking because it made things get bad very fast. I knew how to keep up appearances and function as an alcoholic, but I couldn't do it with drugs."*

Leslie had been clean and sober for a year at the time of the interview. Her father had visited her not long before and was trying to be supportive. After not speaking with her stepmother for ten years, Leslie now talks to her on the phone.

Leslie's recovery is her top priority. When she gets caught up in the excitement of acting, however, it's hard for her to remember that. *"I was doing a shoot last week and my recovery lost its priority. I forgot that I'm not normal, that I'm an addict and an alcoholic."*

Leslie takes part in AA and NA meetings now and finally lets people get to know her. She has found people through the program who are very important to her. And she talks to patients going through the same treatment program she went through. *"Every time I go there, I remember how I felt when I went in. And I know I could end up there again. I'm going through a lot that's common the first year of recovery, but mainly I'm learning to live."* Leslie finds additional support by seeing a therapist who is familiar with twelve-step programs.

Leslie is trying to discover the right spiritual path for herself, one that will work in harmony with her recovery. *"I have my spiritual interests, my program (AA and NA), career, and relationships, but I want to learn how to integrate everything. I don't want them to be separate compartments anymore."*

Life Goals
Leslie plans to live her life one day at a time. Acting is her career focus for now. If she tires of it, she said she has other interests and skills that she can imagine herself pursuing.

Spiritual Beliefs
"I know there's a reason I'm here and there's a path that I'm on. There is something more for me to do, or it would be time for me to leave. I don't know what it is, but I know it will come in God's time, not mine."

Update (January 1990)
Leslie had been clean and sober for a year and nine months. She was still working as an actress and going to four to seven AA or NA meeting a week. She had volunteered to sponsor newcomers at meetings and was spending time answering the AA hotline. And Leslie had bought herself a special gift as part of her recovery and seemed finally to be enjoying her life.

Linda (56, Catholic background, postal service)

Linda was raised as a Catholic and was expected to graduate from college, get married, and raise a family. She read metaphysical books as a child and learned about the Moslem and Jewish religions from men in her life. When she suffered the loss of a fiancé and her two sons, the need for answers led her to metaphysical books and psychics. After many years, she has developed a network of supportive family members and friends who share resources for personal growth and encouragement.

Life Story

Linda's father was Catholic but rarely around when she was growing up because of his naval duties. Linda remembered him as "happy-go-lucky," and she was the only one in the family who kept in touch with him. Her mother, a Chinese Christian, was very serious and strict. She raised her children as Catholics, but followed many Chinese traditions.

Linda was a sickly child and nearly died of pneumonia and later scarlet and rheumatic fever. Her illnesses were one reason her parents sent her to a Catholic boarding school most of her life. As a teenager, she started reading about astrology and numerology.

Linda's family expected her to finish school, get married, and have children. After completing her degree in social science, Linda worked as a social worker until she met and married a Moslem at age twenty-five. She had been a "good Catholic" until then. *"During our relationship, my religious horizons expanded through reading Moslem works. But I didn't agree with their treatment of women."*

Linda had a son, but the marriage didn't last because of the vast differences in their backgrounds and life-styles. Linda left her son with her family and went to New York to work in the theater. *"There I fell in love with a Jewish man who died before we could marry. But I had his son and decided to go home. I knew it would be hard to raise children without a husband, so I took a battery of civil service tests and finally got a job with the postal service."*

After Linda had a daughter with her third husband, she discovered he had an affair. *"He lost his job and didn't tell me. We eventually went through a traumatic divorce. Then my oldest son was diagnosed as having cancer. There I was, alone with three children, one of them dying. I felt like dying myself, but something always kept me going. We tried everything to help my son, including mystics and quacks. One day, a doctor's wife came into my son's hospital room, held my hand and said, 'People are loaned to you.' I have never forgotten that, and I've had to tell other people that."*

Linda's son lived for eighteen months. *"He used to ask me why people have to suffer. I couldn't answer him. I tried to get answers at churches with no luck. Eight months after his death, my second son drowned. I tried looking for answers and then worked at putting my life back together. I knew I had to let go of the past and set my sights on something better for my daughter and me. Then I started reading metaphysical books again."*

Linda discovered and developed her artistic talent and had some showings of her work. Then she decided to go back to school to complete her masters, while still working for the post office.

Linda started going to psychics to get information to find a brother who had disappeared after a nervous breakdown. She worked for ten years trying to find him based on information from several psychics. *"On my daughter's eighteenth birthday, he called me. He had changed his identify and had also been going to psychics. We compared notes and found that the psychics had been telling us the same things about our family and past-life information. The information on our mother's past lives helped us understand her actions in this life."*

In 1975, Linda's mother started suffering a string of illnesses. *"I took her into my house because she didn't want to be put in a home. She was a terror to live with. She tried to control the lives of my daughter and me through superstition. I had to put my life on hold during the ten years I took care of her. A few months before her death, my mother decided to die and refused to eat, starving herself to death. She told me she loved me for the first time just before she died."*

Linda said she grew from the death of her children and mother and from her bother's disappearance. She also credited the different relationships and religions she had been involved in as a crucial part of her growth. *"Every month my daughter and I go to the cemetery with flowers and talk to my sons. We tell them what has been going on with us. I can see a purpose for both my sons lives now. My oldest one made a contribution to medical science as a patient at a teaching hospital and brought love to me. My second son helped me through the illness and death of my first son. I realize now they were meant to be together."*

After her mother died, Linda felt drawn to do something with her hands. She became a certified massage practitioner and studied Reiki and polarity, two forms of energy therapy. *"I have built a network of healers. I have gotten other family members interested in New Age activities and exchange books and tapes with family and friends. I open my doors to many people who are spiritually inclined."* She talks freely about New Age topics at work because several people are interested. *"We go to holistic fairs together. The town is loaded with people who are into metaphysics. I wear crystals and have them in my office."*

Linda is a great networker. She networks for herself and to help her daughter. *"One reason I got involved in New Age was to learn things to help my daughter, who is a precognitive dreamer. I go to classes and meet people who I can call on later. I am learning as many healing arts as I can. I am also a certified hypnotherapist. When I retire from the post office, I may hang out a shingle. Meanwhile, I approach each new topic or technique with a passion and add it to my collection of tools."*

Linda encourages other people not to be afraid of New Age. *"I tell them to play with things in New Age and talk to other people who are involved.*

I enjoy helping people on their path because so many people helped me. I'm not ashamed of being involved in New Age. I believe in God, and I feel comfortable in any church. I've probably been involved with each of them in past lives."

Life Goals

"I know I will use many of the skills I have acquired, but I am not sure what form that will take."

Spiritual Beliefs

"I feel there is a supreme being. I talk to him every day through prayer and meditation. Every morning at breakfast, my daughter and I take turns talking to God. We ask for protection of our house and belongings. We ask for the kind of day we want and thank God for our abundance."

Linda thinks she is in this life for several reasons in addition to her own growth-to foster growth in others, to be a comfort to others, to bring them joy, and to practice her art and healing techniques. *"I listen to the voice or feeling inside me that draws me to new experiences on my spiritual path."*

Intuition, Reason, and Emotion

Linda used to be very emotional. Her anger prompted her to grow and fight for causes. *"I have gone to the ocean and screamed to release emotions. I am much calmer now. I can ask questions about my situation and look at it so that it is not so traumatic. I don't take things as personally anymore or judge anything as totally bad. I want to live, so I don't let things get to me or feel like giving up. I don't want to set that kind of example for my daughter."*

Linda has found she is usually right when she depends on her intuition in hiring people. If she has to decide quickly at work, she uses her intuition; otherwise she takes time to reason over the options.

Growth Techniques

Many years ago, Linda described herself as being a "mousy" person. She wasn't raised to have goals other than being a wife and mother. Her growth came in large part from her meeting the challenges of being the family breadwinner. *"I wouldn't have done a lot of what I have done if it weren't for my daughter. She has been my motivation to learn."*

"At work, I treat my staff and customers the way I would like to be treated. I know that whatever I give out will come back to me. I think my work saved my sanity when I lost my sons."

Linda goes to different psychics depending on her purpose-missing persons, finance, or regression. Sometimes she goes away by herself to get information by tuning into her own Higher Self.

Linda said her life was out of balance when she was the care giver for her mother and daughter. *"I gave up my personal life. When my mother died, I decided to do something for myself and that was traveling. I haven't had any tough times since she died."*

Linda and her relatives keep each other informed of New Age events. *"I find I have surrounded myself with people who have similar interests. We compare notes, share resources, and support each other."*

Martha (68, Episcopal background, psychotherapist)

Martha had spent thirty-three years playing the role of dutiful wife and mother when her husband said he didn't love her anymore and left. She entered group therapy to put the broken pieces of her life back together. What seemed a crisis at the time instead has led her to an exciting career and a very happy second marriage.

Life Story

Even though they weren't particularly religious, Martha's parents sent her and her brothers and sister to Sunday school at a nearby church. Martha's mother was upset, however, when Martha decided to join the Baptist church because her friends were joining.

A few years later, Martha met Paul, a seminary student, and went to the Episcopal church with him. When he completed school, they married and went on to have five children. *"I did everything I thought was expected of a minister's wife. I was at church for all the activities with the children and did volunteer work there. I put the children first, then my husband and his work. But I rarely did anything for myself."*

In the early seventies, Martha took a transactional analysis class to prepare for work as a Weight Watcher lecturer. One day after class, she came home to find her husband had bought a Great Dane without discussing it with her first. Prompted by what she learned in class, she asserted herself for the first time and asked why she hadn't been consulted. *"I was beginning to realize that I had trained my family to expect unreasonable things from me and to take me for granted. I knew I deserved more than I had been giving myself. As I read more and more, my self-esteem began to increase."*

Martha said her husband had never been very open or emotional during their marriage. A month after the transactional analysis workshop, her husband asked to meet her at his church. *"When I got there, no one was there. I found him at a restaurant with two of our adult children. I could tell something was wrong with the children, but Paul made up an excuse and took me back to the church. I thought he was going to tell me that he wanted out of the ministry."*

After thirty-three years of being a dutiful and sacrificing wife, Martha learned instead that her husband wanted a divorce. He had just told his children at dinner. *"My first reaction was to laugh. I thought he was trying something out on me before counseling someone in the church."* But Martha quickly realized he was serious. When she asked why, he said he had fallen out of love with her five years earlier. She couldn't believe he had felt this way and had never discussed it with her. He left her soon after.

Martha entered group therapy to pull the pieces of her life together and to try to discover what her part in it had been. *"I learned that I was over-adaptive and didn't look out for myself. Whenever I wanted intimacy from my husband, he pulled away, and I went along with that."*

Once her roles of wife and mother were gone, Martha had no idea who she was. *"I grew up believing that men were more important than women, that women were supposed to serve their family and do everything to make the marriage work and keep the family together."* Martha's husband came from a family background full of broken marriages. When Martha and Paul broke up, he told her that if he had married anyone else, it wouldn't have lasted five years.

Now Martha looks at the end of her marriage as a blessing. *"If it had continued, I might not have discovered myself or grown as much as I have. And I would have continued to deny my own needs."*

The benefits Martha received from therapy planted the seed that she would like to do the same type of work some day. Within a year, she enrolled in college to finish her bachelor's degree. She eventually earned credentials in transactional analysis and certification in Neuro-Linguistic Programming[13] (NLP).

About the time she started back to school, Martha met a man whom she dated for three years and has been married to for over eleven years. *"Our relationship is a real partnership, including making business decisions together."* Martha's husband taught her to fly, and she soloed at age fifty-nine. *"I'm truly happy, living a life in which work, recreation, and relationships are evenly balanced."*

---

13. NLP is the study of internal and external communications. NLP research, based chiefly on the work of Richard Bandler and John Grinder, has resulted in several techniques whose aim is to help people get what they want from life by expanding their choices regarding perception, thinking, feeling, and behavior.

During her earlier years as wife and mother, Martha spent many hours as a chauffeur and would say, *"God, surely you have something more planned for me."* Now she sees those times as a training ground for her work as a therapist. She cares about people and loves her work. *"I'd probably do it even if I didn't get paid. I don't even try to get clients. When people are ready to make changes in their lives, they call me. And I think I have more spiritual discussions with people now than I did as a minister's wife."*

Spiritual Beliefs

Martha says no one is stagnant, they are either growing or dying. For her, growing spiritually is finding out why she's here and what God's plan is for her. She believes that part of her purpose is to discover and hone her talents and offer them in a way that will serve others. Another purpose is to be more loving. *"God put us here to learn how to get along with each other."*

Martha believes in changing people by being a model of her beliefs rather than trying to convince them of her beliefs. *"We each have to find our own way of teaching how to become enlightened."*

Martha still believes in the Trinity she learned in church. To her, they are: *"God, the Father, who created the world; God, the son Jesus, who came as a model of what we could be; and when God could not be everywhere at once, he left us His Holy Spirit."*

Growth Techniques

Therapy has been very important in Martha's growth. She also credits reading, meditation, learning from her clients, and networking with people in her profession.

The Future

Martha is optimistic that the desire for peace will continue to grow. She believes that people are willing to make sacrifices to maintain peace and protect the environment. She has undertaken to learn more about promoting peace, recycling, saving fuel and energy, and sharing what she has learned with others.

That which makes you feel separate tends to keep your life from working effectively, and that which enables YOU to experience love and unity permits you to harmonize your energy with the energies of the world around you. Whenever you are in doubt about whether to do something or not, just ask yourself *whether it makes you feel more separate from people or more loving toward people.*

- Handbook to Higher Consciousness

6   Guided to New Age

The people is this category came to New Age as adults without the catalyst of an outside crisis and often without prior spiritual awareness. They reached a point in their lives where they felt that something was missing and in their search for it stumbled upon New Age books, people, or seminars. For some, the search was triggered by their first mystical experience. But they all felt it was time for their spiritual awakening and that they were led to the resources they needed by their Soul, Higher Self, or God.

Whatever the reason, the result was that their emptiness began to be filled and questions were answered. And they wanted more. Those without a strong spiritual background felt as if they had found God for the first time. They were suddenly thinking and saying things about spiritual matters they wouldn't have believed possible only a short time before. They found beliefs and experiences that finally gave meaning to their lives.

Marilyn (65, Episcopal background, retired professor)

Although Marilyn grew up in a Catholic and Episcopal family, by graduate school she was an atheist. She married an atheist and raised her children to be the same. But at age fifty, she had a series of experiences which forced her to reclaim her spirituality.

Life Story

Marilyn grew up with two religions-her father and brother were Catholic while she and her mother were Episcopalian. She learned early that religion was serious but saw there was no single, simple truth since her parents couldn't agree.

When Marilyn first read about Buddhism at age fifteen, she wondered whether Christianity was the "right" religion or if she had become involved by chance. *"When I mentioned that at home, the roof blew off. My parent's reaction was so frightening that I didn't pursue it with them. But I always read and talked about philosophy."*

During high school and college, Marilyn dropped pieces of her religious beliefs. By graduate school, where she was training to become an experimental psychologist, Marilyn was preaching atheism. *"That seemed wonderfully clean to me. I was always an ethical person and felt strongly about social responsibility and was involved in social and political action. But without a spiritual life, it was a burden to think I had to do it all on my own."*

After graduate school, Marilyn married and took a job teaching in a college. A week after her first baby was born, a book she had written was published with several errors. *"I went into a serious depression and was on a waiting list for a bed in a hospital psychiatric unit. I asked myself what life would be like after being in the hospital. I knew the same problems would exist. The only difference would be that my medical history would show I had been in a mental hospital. I didn't think that would be very helpful, so I decided not to go into the hospital and to get over the depression myself. I couldn't stop feeling depressed, but I could stop acting depressed."* Marilyn eventually came out of the depression with the help of a psychiatrist she had been seeing about some family problems.

Two years later, just when Marilyn was getting funding for a program she had initiated, her husband said he wanted to move to another city. After moving, Marilyn had two children and no household help, so she couldn't work, which she greatly missed.

When Marilyn finally found someone to care for the children, she decided to do postdoctoral work to become a clinical psychologist. *"I loved the clinical work and found that doing therapy with others helped me to grow."*

When she finished the program, however, Marilyn went back to teaching instead of clinical work. *"I found a small college outside a big city with a devoted faculty and some wonderful students. Some of the students were from a Roman Catholic seminary nearby, and I became friends with them because they were so open to new ideas."*

In her second year at the college, Marilyn taught a course that opened up the old philosophical questions she had set aside years before.

"*Suddenly I had to look at free will, determinism, morality, ethics, and holism versus reductionism. And I truly enjoyed it.*"

In early December of that year, her parents came to visit. Marilyn's mother gave her a record of folk-type singing by Benedictine monks. "*When I listened to it, I was blown away by what I heard. I played the record over and over. The first words were, 'Anything happens if we are open.'*"

Her seminarian friends invited her to a Christmas party about a week later. "*It was fabulous because people weren't playing games as they did at academic parties. I told one of my students that he had something very special there. He answered, 'It's God.' I opened my mouth to make a joke, but the words from the record went through my mind, and I told him he just may be right.*"

Then very dramatic things happened inside Marilyn's mind. "*A dialogue started about why I said that and what is God. One side of my mind reviewed all my college philosophy courses. I asked what those guys had there. I answered, 'Love.' Then I said, 'You mean love is God?'*"

Marilyn started that night trying to put together those two concepts of God and love. "*I saw that anyone could know love. You didn't have to have a PhD; in fact, that may interfere with it.*"

Marilyn's drive home from the party became a magical experience, with a new appreciation for the Christmas lights and scenery. "*I couldn't think about it over the weekend with my family around. And I wasn't ready to talk about it. I hadn't turned from an atheist to a believer, but something wonderful was happening.*"

A few days later, when Marilyn was alone, the dialogue in her head began again. She heard answers in the form of biblical quotations. "*I wondered where all the Bible stuff was coming from. I didn't want to deal with all that Christianity stuff. When I asked myself who Jesus was, the answer was that Jesus was the 'embodiment' of love, the 'incarnation.' When I thought about the word 'incarnation,' the whole body of Christian doctrine I had learned came back to me and fit into place like a jigsaw puzzle. It became a part of me. I saw that the Communion of Saints meant the fellowship of all those who are living in the energy of love. That was a tremendous experience for me.*"

By that night, Marilyn was ready to say she was a Christian. "*It was a little painful and thrilling. I had to say it to my husband and my parents. Amazing things happened in my relationships with other people. People who knew me only slightly sensed something different in me and responded accordingly. It was as if I had a glow, and people were responding to it. The anger I had carried shifted into clean assertiveness. And I shifted from being harried to letting a loving universe take care of things.*"

In her general psychology classes, when Marilyn taught about emotions, she started with love instead of fear and anger as she had before. "*I found I had to integrate more and more of my new spirituality into* my teaching. I didn't feel so removed from my students because of their religious backgrounds. My new interest in the spiritual and religious eventually contributed to my early retirement from teaching psychology."

Marilyn's husband thought she had gone crazy. "He asked if my new religion was anti-sex, and I assured him it wasn't. I told him it added a spiritual experience to the physical one. That was hard for him to understand. And I wanted to be around more people who knew what I was experiencing, but my husband didn't want any part of it. Eventually, we separated and then divorced."

Marilyn was happy to have found some loving Roman Catholic communities which welcomed her doubts and questions and supported her learning and growth. When she moved to another part of the country, however, she didn't feel comfortable with any of the traditional churches. She liked some of the clergy, but not the traditions and lack of mysticism.

Now Marilyn calls herself an "eclectic Christian." "I feel as if I'm sitting in a void. There's no specific set of spiritual beliefs that I call my own. (Carl) Jung talked about the individuated, mature person being able to tolerate the tension between opposite poles without coming down on either side. I have had some experiences that felt like that, and it's the most painful place in the world to be. That's the void I sit in now."

Her new spiritual beliefs led her to live with a Nicaraguan family for a month, to be arrested for civil disobedience, and to go back to Nicaragua a second time for "the scariest experience of my life." In a simple way, Marilyn wants to act out the "radical" Christianity that says other people are her sisters and brothers and that she has some responsibility for them. "It has to do with the immanence of God and the siblinghood of humankind. I don't talk about it very much; I just try to live it."

Marilyn wishes she had a clear vision of what is ahead for her so she could feel she was directing her life. "I'm living a responsive and reactive life, waiting to see what the universe brings my way. So far it has brought memberships on the board of directors of some growth and retreat centers, and I work with Psychologists for Social Responsibility. I have the time and money to do what I want, but I've been unable to find that one thing to commit to."

Life Goals

Marilyn feels she wants too much. "I would like to be an artist, scholar, or therapist, but I'm not sure I would be good enough at any of them. I may write a book about my journey. But that would mean putting aside some of my other activities, which would be hard because of my old Puritan conscience that makes me feel the need to serve."

Spiritual Beliefs

Marilyn doesn't believe any human concept of God can be accurate, because it would be too limiting.

She doesn't believe in one set of standard morals or ethics that spiritually developed people should follow. *"I think it's an internal thing for each person. You have to wait for social activism to come from inside."*

Marilyn believes in a dark and light side in everyone, and she cherishes both of hers. She thinks people should look for and acknowledge their dark side and integrate it within themselves.

As a scientist, Marilyn looked at reincarnation as a model of life whose usefulness could be explored, rather than as a theory to be proved true or false. *"I wondered how it would affect me to act as if reincarnation were a fact. I decided babies would be more interesting, that I would feel more responsible for my life, and that I would have reason to learn from younger people. I decided to try living as if the model of reincarnation were true. If it is, then all experience is part of a learning process which I can take with me when I go. Since I love learning, I continue to use reincarnation as a working model even though I have no idea whether it's true or not."*

Growth Techniques

Marilyn takes time to read spiritual or religious material each morning. Two books she recommends are *The Reenchantment of Science* and *Spirituality & Society*, both edited by David R. Griffin.

Now Marilyn meditates only when she feels the need to center herself, especially when she has several things going at once. *"I recently chaired a committee meeting where I had everyone spend five minutes in silent meditation to bring themselves fully into the moment. They thanked me at the end, and said they didn't realize how much they needed it."*

Marilyn has practiced yoga for ten years and has gone to retreats at a Buddhist meditation center. She has also taken advantage of massage, rolfing[1], and psychosynthesis[2] workshops.

---

1. Rolfing. A series of bodywork sessions which aim for structural alignment and balance through deep tissue manipulation. The process was founded by Ida P. Rolf.
2. Psychosynthesis is a form of transpersonal psychology developed by Roberto Assagioli in the 1920's. Transpersonal psychology recognizes spiritual realities. In addition to the conscious self, psychosynthesis recognizes the existence of the "Higher Self," a spiritual consciousness.

Bob (30, Lutheran background, teacher/musician)

Bob grew up with a suicidal mother who couldn't accept being divorced. Bob recently realized how much he was influenced by his mother's sense of insecurity and fear of relationships. The spiritual approach to teaching developed by Maria Montessori was the catalyst for beginning his process of self-healing.

Life Story

Even though both of Bob's parents were raised as Lutherans, religion wasn't discussed at home. Bob went to Lutheran Bible classes every Sunday until tenth grade, when he went through confirmation. Then he stopped going regularly and quit completely after high school. *"I went to church out of a sense of obligation rather than curiosity or wanting to learn."*

Bob said he didn't have strong memories of his early childhood, except that he felt his family had been happy. Bob's parents divorced, however, when he was eleven, and his brothers, sister, and he stayed with his mother.

Both his parents remarried soon after, but Bob's mother's marriage lasted only a year. *"For many years, my mother was on the verge of suicide because she blamed herself for the divorce and not being able to keep a father around for us. We tried to convince her that she had done a good job raising us, but she wouldn't believe us."*

During his senior year in college, Bob discovered that he and his major in computers were not compatible. *"I knew I wanted to work with people, not machines. But I went ahead and finished my degree."* Once he started working in the computer field, he realized something about computers appealed to him and he was good at it. He was also happy that it was a well paying career even though he felt spoiled by all the money he was making.

After a while, Bob's desire to work with people prompted him to seek a career change, so he moved to California and went back to college. He started as a music major and took a variety of other courses. He also became strongly involved in the peace movement on campus. *"I couldn't do enough; I protested and got arrested several times. I appeared to be peaceful, but I would get angry with people, and a friend called me on it. I didn't realize until then that I was asking the world to be peaceful while I had an incredible war going on inside myself.*" Bob called that a major turning point and was finally open to knowing the truth about himself.

Bob continued to ask himself what career would allow him to apply his skills and gifts in an effort that would be more meaningful to him and the world. The answer he got was to work with children to prepare them to be the foundation for tomorrow. *"I knew I couldn't work in public schools using the traditional approaches, so I went to a Montessori school and was impressed by the children and the fact that the teacher was not the main figure in the classroom. I read a book the teacher gave me on Montessori and knew that was for me."*

Bob said that his Montessori training awakened spiritual ideas in him because Maria Montessori considered each child as a whole being whose spirit needed to be nourished, along with the intellect. Bob learned to nourish the spirit by respecting it and to be a guide and mirror for the children, reflecting their beauty and perfection.

Bob has been working as a preschool teacher for a few years and has used his experience to acquaint himself with his own inner child. *"I learned to look through the eyes of a child and to experience that same simplicity in approaching life and extending unconditional love for others."*

Bob hasn't been involved in spiritual groups, but has a few friends with whom he shares experiences and discusses spiritual lessons they each face. Bob can also share his beliefs with one of his brothers and his sister. While the rest of his family may not agree with what he does or thinks, Bob feels that they respect him for doing what he feels he has to do. *"That means a lot to me. I think my family benefits from my growth, and I feel closer to them now than I ever have."*

Bob has been singing and playing guitar for about eight years and knows he will continue with that very important part of his life. *"I've written twenty songs and feel that a lot more are coming. As I mature spiritually, I feel my creativity becoming more open and free."*

A short time before the interview, Bob was laid off his teaching job because of a lack of funding. Since he feels that his life's purpose is to serve children, he plans to get his certificate for teaching older children.

Spiritual Beliefs

Bob doesn't concern himself with how we got here. *"I don't want to spend a lot of energy on whether or not it's an illusion. The concept of reincarnation helps me be more accepting of myself and my growth, but I'm not interested in pursuing past lives."*

Bob sees the ultimate destination for each person as being one with God or the perfect being. And he allows that there are many paths one may take to get there. *"No one outside me has all the answers or the right way for me. There is no right way or wrong way, only an appropriate or inappropriate way for each individual to find the truth."*

Bob follows two spiritual rituals regularly, at meals and before bed. At meal time, he centers himself into the present moment with a deep breath. *"I do that so I can fully appreciate the fact that I am giving myself life. On the second breath in, I visualize earth, air, fire, and water because they are what give me life. On the second breath out, I cleanse the food, releasing anything that is not natural, like chemicals and preservatives. On the third breath, I breathe in the love that went into preparing it and the nutrition in it. On the breath out, I give thanks and feel it giving me life."*

Before bed, Bob sits before a small altar in his room and meditates, focusing on his breath and repeating a mantra. *"I let go of any thoughts that come in and meditate between ten and thirty minutes. I do it no matter how tired I am. To finish up, I use three deep breaths to release anything that isn't of the here and now so that when I lie down, I'm not carrying thoughts of the past or future."* Staying in the present is what allows him to stay at peace.

Bob appreciates the practice in India where people greet others by saying *"Namaste,"* which he said means, *"I honor the place in you wherein lies your uniqueness, peace, beauty, perfection, and godliness. When you are in that place in you and I am in that place in me, there is only one of us."*

Growth Techniques

Bob doesn't spend much time looking for more resources outside himself. Instead, he focuses on applying the principles he has learned to everyday life events. In particular, he works at creating peace in the world by creating it in himself first. *"I feel that developing peace in myself has done more good than running around working on peace causes with the anger I used to have inside. I interact with many people everyday and influence them through the feelings I carry. My feelings used to be anger, rejection, and impatience which can feed negative feelings in others. I know that the feelings of love that I carry now can be healing to the people I meet."*

Bob knows that becoming aware of an issue is the first step to working through it. *"I recently realized I have an incredible fear of hurting any woman with whom I'm involved. I'm afraid she will go through what my mother did. I'm slow in ending relationships that aren't working because I don't want to hurt the woman. Now that I am aware of that, I can grow past it."*

Another realization was about how insecure Bob was, just like his mother. Although he had done well in school and was successful on his own, he assumed the worst when someone wanted to talk to him at work. *"Doubting myself violates my belief that a perfect being is inside me. It's my choice to stay in that old behavior or to stop practicing it."*

Once Bob experiences a better way, he can't go back to the old way. He gave sex as an example because he now considers it as much a spiritual experience as a physical one. *"I can't imagine meeting a woman in a bar and having casual sex. It would be such a big step back for me. I see that going on around me, but I don't fight it anymore or shake my head and wonder when they will get their act together. I smile at it and know that they too are on their path."*

Bob loves the grin on the Buddha. *"I've been told he is grinning because he knows it is all so simple. And yet we make it so difficult."*

Jean (63, no religious background, retired nurse)

Jean's parents turned away from their religion before she was born. She grew up without love and learned to fear everything. As a wife and mother, her need for power and absolute control were overwhelming. Finally, a friend gave her a book that started her on the road to loving herself and her family.

Life Story
Jean's parents had been fundamentalist missionaries before she was born. On a foreign mission, her father became ill and then had a nervous breakdown when he and his wife's lives were threatened. Jean said her father lost faith, not because of the threats, but because he felt God had let him down. Her parents came home, had a family, and never discussed religion again.

Jean said her parents exercised absolute control over their children. *"We would never think of talking back to them. I was afraid of my parents and everything else. Even though I wouldn't show my fear to them, all my dreams were full of fear."*

Jean coped with her overwhelming sense of fear by putting on a happy face for the world and pretending that everything was fine. *"I did everything perfectly so no one could criticize me. And I felt the need to have control over everybody. I was terrified if I didn't."*

Jean's teenage years were marked by confusion and rebellion. At eighteen, she took a ride with a stranger who had a gun and tried to kidnap her. She jumped out of the moving car, suffering a concussion, but she managed to hide until he left. Getting no sympathy at home was the last straw.

She wanted to leave home, but she also wanted to be safe, so she married her brother-in-law. *"I had three children, and I needed absolute obedience from them in order to feel in control. I panicked if they even looked like they were going to talk back to me. I thought that was how you raised children.*"

After a few years, Jean began to feel restless. She was tired of being "so good" for other people all her life. She said her husband felt the same way, so they had a couple of "wild years" before their marriage ended.

After another wild period on her own, Jean married again because she didn't feel she could earn enough to support herself and her children. But she still recognized her need for control and power. A friend gave her a book titled, *The Power of Positive Thinking*, by Norman Vincent Peale. "*With the word 'power,' I thought it would be great. When I read the word 'God,' I set the book aside. But the word 'power' finally drew me back to the book. I decided to pretend there was a God so I could get the power.*"

Jean said that until that time she had never felt love for anyone, not even her children. She had been the only person that mattered. The book suggested that she try to feel love for the two people she disliked the most. "*That was my sister and father. I worked at what the book said, and it became almost a game. I finally felt love for my sister. It took longer to feel love for my father, but one afternoon I did, for the first time in my life.*"

Later that same afternoon, Jean was in the kitchen and felt love radiating through her. She noticed a blazing light in the corner of the kitchen. She could only look to the side of it because it was so bright. "*It stretched from the ceiling to the floor. I kept feeling the love radiating. I could feel the heat from the light in the muscles and bones of my hand. My children came running into the kitchen wanting me to settle a quarrel. They were struck not by the light but by looking at me. They immediately started grinning and looked lovingly at each other. I put my hand out towards my daughter. The only way I can describe what happened is that solid love came down my arm, left my body, and when it touched my daughter, I felt as if I was touching her. Then the kids tiptoed out looking very happy. When I turned back, the light was gone. I don't have any memories from then until I saw my husband later that evening.*"

The next day Jean thought she was either insane or had had a spiritual experience. She didn't want either one to be true, so she avoided thinking about it for six weeks. Then she wanted to know if she was insane, so she started reading everything she could find that might have the answer. After reading the Bible and several other books, Jean felt reassured that other people had had the same experience and decided that it was a spiritual one.

Her husband became upset when he saw her reading the Bible. He accused her of thinking she was better than he was. He turned cruel towards Jean and the children and threatened to kill them. Jean had to put him in a mental hospital when he threatened to kill himself.

Jean described herself as having a lot of psychic power at that time. One example involved her cats who had been fighting in the basement. When she went down, she found one of the kittens with a serious wound on it abdomen. *"I felt such love for that kitten and felt so helpless. I thought, OK, there's a power greater than I am. I picked up the kitten and felt love for it. I lost sense of time, but then I felt a release and put the kitten down and went back upstairs. I was glowing with love. After the glow calmed down, I realized I didn't even check the kitten. When I went back down, I found one with hair going inside the body along the line of the tear. There was no scar. I assumed the tear had closed so quickly that the hair had gotten caught in it. I thanked God for the miracle and added, 'But you could have made it neater.'"* Jean said that several similar experiences have happened to her. But while she admitted she enjoyed using the power, she was glad she didn't get carried away with it.

She also has learned to communicate with her guidance to help her make decisions. She always asks for the highest and tells her guidance to "stop" her if she is wrong. When she gets stopped, she knows she is going in the wrong direction. She had a very physical example of that when she had decided to ask a support group for advice about her husband who was still in the mental hospital. Every time she opened her mouth to say something, someone else cut her off. *"I thought, 'Next time I'm going to say it real fast. Stop me if I'm wrong.' The next time there was a pause, I opened my mouth and felt an invisible fist come in my mouth and down my throat. I thought, 'OK, OK, don't be so rough.' I realized then that I wasn't supposed to ask them."*

Jean finally decided to give her husband a divorce and went on welfare with her four children. Based on an aptitude test, Jean enrolled in nursing school. She went to school, worked a part-time job, took care of her children, and eventually graduated with honors, happy that she was able to support her family.

After she started working, she had another unusual experience. She woke up at noon one day to find herself fully dressed at work. She had done all her paperwork and had attended the monthly meeting. She had no memory of what had happened, but felt that strong sense of love again. When a couple of patients came up to her, she knew everything they were going to say before they said it. *"I responded without thinking about my answers. The words just came out. I made a phone call without knowing the number. I said what I had to say and put the phone down. Then I recognized my first thought since waking up which was, 'This is strange, but I'm not sure I can stay like this.' I thought it felt wonderful knowing everything."* After a few days, Jean began to feel bored with knowing everything and missed the normal sensation of her body. A few days later, the love feeling was gone, and she and her body felt normal again. She was afraid it would happen again and didn't want to take risks with her patients, so she quit her job.

She found other nursing positions she felt comfortable with and a few years later realized what had happened. *"I went into another reality, a knowing reality. It was similar to the feelings of love and knowing I often had in medical crises, except they lasted only a few minutes. But that time, it happened with no clear stimulus."*

Jean began recording the days when she woke up feeling love vibrating throughout her body. She found that it usually happened the day after the critical point on her biorhythm emotional cycle.

In medical crises, she learned to empty herself, ask for guidance, and then wait for some power to work through her. Many times she didn't know what she had done for the patient until later. But she said it always turned out perfectly. *"I can't seem to use this power unless there is some strong emotion like anxiety, fear, or frustration that makes me give up. I keep thinking there must be some way to give up without having something horrible happen."*

Jean hasn't told her children about her oppressive childhood or her few "wild times." She started to tell them once because she thought they would have more insight into their own problems. But the ones she thought she could help didn't want to hear.

Jean has one brother who understands and supports what she is doing. She also has a support group which she treasures because they're open to discussing spiritual topics.

Now that she is retired and lives alone, Jean tries to balance her day with work and play. She reads for a few hours in the morning, spends time on her chores, and then plays in the afternoon. She especially likes spending time in the woods by herself.

Parenting

Jean's spiritual pursuits have helped her to finally feel love for her children. She can see how she tried to break their will and control them before. *"When I became aware of what I was doing, I realized that my children still wanted me to take their power, to do everything for them. I had to break them of that gently so they could take responsibility for their own lives. I look forward to their having the courage to talk back to me."*

Life Goals

There are times when Jean would like to live in the woods by herself. But she feels she should be available in case her children need help. She would like to get married again but feels it would be hard to find someone with similar spiritual interests.

Spiritual Beliefs

Jean believes that each person creates her own image of God depending on her beliefs. For some, God is loving, for others, He is punishing. Jean believes in a loving God that she can't know completely using only her brain. *"I know there is some connection between God and me. When I empty myself, I feel another energy flowing through me. I believe who I really am is just taking a ride on the physical body. Even though we feel separate from each other in our bodies, I think we are all one at some level. Feeling that oneness with everyone is my goal."*

Growth Techniques

Jean has used reading as a primary source of spiritual instruction. She started with the Bible and then several of Mary Baker Eddy's books. *"I have books everywhere. I feel that books try to reach me as much as I try to reach them. I have often walked through libraries and bookstores knowing I'll be led to the right book. And it always works."*

Jean has spent time at a Tibetan institute where she learned to recognize and overcome spiritual blocks. She has been going to spiritual retreats for thirty years and has visited several communes in the hopes of finding the right one to join. *"I haven't found the place that's right for me yet. I would love to have a place of my own in the woods for spiritual people to go. It feels so good being with people who understand and support what you're doing."*

Update (December 1989)

Jean wrote that she felt drawn to visit ashrams in India and had made plans to go there for four months in 1990.

Jeff (37, Catholic background, finance executive)

Jeff has lived a quiet life and enjoyed his early Catholic experiences. He carefully planned every aspect of his life until he had a good job, family, house, and car. But a sense that something was missing led him to metaphysical books which turned his belief system upside down. He has been lucky to have a spouse who supports and joins him in his gradual, stable process of spiritual growth.

Life Story

Jeff considered his childhood uneventful, even boring. His daily routine was going to Catholic school, practicing piano, doing homework, and going to bed. He enjoyed his church involvement as an altar and choirboy.

As he got older, Jeff began to cut his ties with the church. *"I saw the hypocrisy and how rules changed. I became more aware of what role religion played in history. It seemed to be a more manipulative than spiritual force. I tried some 'born again' Christian churches, but they didn't feel right either."*

While at college, Jeff met his future wife. *"I always looked for the safe way to do things, preparing, and planning ahead. So I knew I had to find a job before I could marry."* Jeff worked part-time at a bank while in school and took a full-time job in banking after graduation. A few months later, Jeff felt prepared for marriage. He used the same careful planning approach in buying a house and having children.

Jeff and his wife planned to raise their children in an organized religion and then let them decide what to do later. *"We tried the Roman Catholic church and went as far as communion with our daughter. But the church expected the parents to be involved. Their attempt at control pushed me away from it again. Now my children don't go to any church. But they see us live our beliefs and that we're calmer and have fewer arguments."*

While Jeff followed all the rules to material success and had a house, car, children, and a good job, he had a need that went unsatisfied. *"My boss thought I would stay there forever. But there were things I wanted to do that I couldn't do there. My wife and I realized we were in a rut, and we didn't even like the area we lived in. So we started researching other places to live."*

About the same time, Jeff started listening to a nightly radio talk show that discussed metaphysical topics. *"I heard an author talk about reincarnation and went to the library to get her book. That was the first metaphysical book I read. Then I came across the Seth[3] books. My wife and I read them aloud at night and discussed them. Although we were suspicious at first, we decided to take the information for what it was worth and not be concerned about the source."*

The concept of creating one's own reality, as discussed in the Seth books, had quite an influence on Jeff. *"It took about three months to make the break from the Roman Catholic God and shift our beliefs from 'why did this happen to me' to 'why did I cause it to happen.' You keep wanting to go back to holding someone else responsible. Then you come back to the idea that you caused it for a reason. I read that everything can be a stumbling block or a stepping*

---

3. Seth is a non-physical entity or energy personality who channeled several metaphysical books through Jane Roberts starting in the late 1960's.

stone, depending on how you look at it. After we assimilated the belief that we were responsible and could really feel it, we knew we had to do something about it. Then we had the nerve to move."

Jeff thought about his requirements for a new job and decided he wanted to have fewer responsibilities and feel more relaxed. After several months of searching and making contacts in their chosen city, Jeff found a job in finance. "*After a few weeks, my boss gave me an opportunity to do something exciting that I hadn't done before. I couldn't have planned that. The new job worked out better than I hoped. It gave me evidence that I didn't have to have everything planned out for things to turn out well.*"

While Jeff was on his own for a few months, waiting for his family to sell the house and move, he started going to the library, picking up books that felt right to him. "*Reading has been the major source of new information for me. When my family moved here, I was able to discuss what I read with my wife, and we have supported each other in our growth. It was annoying at first when one of us said to the other, 'Why did you cause that?' But we noticed after we assimilated the reasons why, we had less headaches, colds, and sickness.*"

Jeff has become more balanced in his attitude towards work. "*When I need a break, I take one. I don't force myself to work late or stress myself out because I know my body will force me to relax by getting a cold. And when I avoid thinking about something that I don't like, I get a headache. As I face those things more, I have fewer headaches.*"

Jeff heard about *A Course in Miracles*[4] and bought the books. His wife read them often and with comparative ease, but Jeff had to work hard at getting through each page because of the challenge to his beliefs the material contained. Jeff continues to find himself drawn from one book or subject to another. "*My wife and I have some interests in common and explore others on our own. Having different interests allows us to get contrasting opinions on things. But we are supportive of our individual paths.*"

Jeff said that his parents and relatives aren't interested in his spiritual beliefs. "*My parents think I'm involved in the devil's work. They keep waiting for God to bring me around. I can't convince them that I will be OK in this, so I try to live my beliefs rather than preach them.*"

Jeff is happy to be living away from his relatives because so many holidays and weekends were taken up with family commitments. "*Now our weekends are free, and we can be more spontaneous. I can't stand spending time doing something I don't like. Living away from our families has turned out even*

---

4. *A Course in Miracles* is a three part set of books that was channeled by an unidentified voice (belived to be Christ) to an atheistic research psychologist over a seven year period starting in 1965. The books consist of a Textbook, a Workbook for Students consisting of 365 daily lessons, and a Manual for Teachers.

better than we imagined. Now my parents come down for a few days to visit, and we have a good time."

Parenting

Jeff feels that he has only temporary custody of his children, preparing them for their own lives. *"Accepting that I create my own reality means that when I come home, I try not to blame my family for anything that went wrong that day. My beliefs make parenting less stressful, and I can laugh about problems."*

Spiritual Beliefs

Jeff finds it hard to put his concept of God into words because it would be too limiting. *"I don't know if it's a separate being or the composite of energy that runs through all of us. I don't think it's something that controls or punishes me."*

"Dark forces are the culmination of negativity in all of us. If a group of people believe they are going to make black magic, they will. A belief can create just about anything."

Growth Techniques

Jeff credits his growth mainly to books and life experiences. *"I notice the subtle changes in myself-more relaxed, open, and flexible. I have a feeling that if I didn't change on a gradual, even basis, something sudden would happen to force change."*

A Course in Miracles helped Jeff stop striking back at people when they strike at him. *"I look at their attack as a fear reaction, not an attack on me. Instead of striking back, I wonder what's bothering them to cause that. It takes a lot of awareness and restraint to react that way."*

At work, Jeff discovered that people can take on more responsibilities if he looks for what they do right, rather than criticize what they do wrong. *"It helps keep me open-minded. I find people asking for more work and suggesting creative ways to do things. It's my decision whether or not to let a situation get out of control."*

"My spiritual growth has been a subtle, even, relaxing experience that has enhanced my life. In all fairness, I don't know if I'm at this point because of my age or because of my experiences. Some of what has happened to me may be typical of people my age."

Paula (36, atheistic background, past-life therapist)

Paula grew up in Europe as an atheist. She moved to the United States after college and worked as a counselor. At twenty-five, she committed to her spiritual growth after experiencing and training to do past-life regressions. Her spiritual insights have led her to focus on the present and to look inward for answers that bring balance and harmony to her life.

Life Experiences

Paula was born in Poland to spiritual parents who didn't believe in God. She said her parents love nature and harmony and don't take advantage of people, but they believe God is a fairy tale. Paula spent some time in France in her late teens and met people involved in Christian charismatic movements. She felt close to them and saw they were inspired by something she didn't understand.

In 1974, after college, Paula came to the United States to teach French. She went back to college and earned a masters in social work. At twenty-five, she trained to do past-life regressions. Entranced and moved by the training, she consciously started on her spiritual journey. *"It was an incredible one hundred eighty degree switch for me to go from being an atheist to saying maybe there was a God. I had to allow myself to be one of the naive types my parents said believed in that fairy tale."*

While Paula worked as a psychotherapist and counselor, she read and studied several spiritual books. *"Raymond Moody's Life After Life brought me to tears and to a strong connection with life beyond what is visible."* She studied *A Course in Miracles*[5] and read about yogis and books by Ruth Montgomery. She feels she was supposed to come to a spiritual awakening by herself in this lifetime. *"Having no religious training in childhood left me free to go anyway I wanted to as an adult. An unconscious current or deep knowing seemed to lead me, and my rational beliefs finally gave way."*

When Paula started on her path, she saw a psychic who told her this would be her last or next to last lifetime. Suddenly, her spiritual interests

---

5. *A Course in Miracles* is a three part set of books that was channeled by an unidentified voice (belived to be Christ) to an atheistic research psychologist over a seven year period starting in 1965. The books consist of a Textbook, a Workbook for Students consisting of 365 daily lessons, and a Manual for Teachers.

and pursuits exploded. She read books, tried to meditate, and set a spiritual ideal as her life's goal. She wanted to get as close to that ideal as she could, and then she hoped she would be finished.

For about five years, her path was a solitary one, finding few people who understood or supported her search. A psychic told her that the period was a karmic situation of her own choice allowing her to resolve some problems and to know herself better.

In early 1988, Paula said that sense of karma lifted almost overnight. Friendships and spiritual resources came back into her life. Although she felt rejected at first during those years, she had learned to depend on and love herself. Now if she has a problem, she doesn't have to run to someone for help.

Not long after, Paula married and then had two children, presenting her a dilemma about their spiritual training. Paula decided not to push her spiritual beliefs on her children. She knows she will have to introduce her ideas to her children at some point because her ideas are so important to her. But she wants to introduce her children to a church for the social advantages and group support, and it is also important to Paula to find a church that will make her children feel good about themselves.

She is excited about the opportunity her children have given her to focus and express her love. *"Every day they give me the chance to be more loving and happy. Children are truly God's gift to people to grow and become more creative and flexible."*

Since having her children, she focuses her limited work schedule to past-life regressions and therapy, and most of her clients have some spiritual interest. Some want to learn a little and move on to other practices or techniques. Some want to use regression as a serious tool in their growth. *"One of the greatest things past-life regression can do for people is help them realize that they are not just this limited body. It is more than the intellectual information you get from a psychic. People can really experience some other lifetime they've had. Not only does the fear of death disappear for them, but a greater scope of what the soul is opens up. It's amazing how it opens up the sense of being eternal and how fun it all is."* She said that some of her clients aren't able to remember past lives because of subconscious fears or blocks. During regressions, she said a few of her clients have remembered their first lifetime on this planet, coming here from other planets or dimensions to continue their growth in a new environment.

By doing regressions on herself, Paula discovered she is in a very high-strung body. She said she wouldn't have realized it if she hadn't recalled other lifetimes that were very peaceful and balanced.

Describing her spiritual path as a process of ebb and flow, Paula said she was in an ebbing phase, regrouping and reexamining her beliefs. She was formulating a new philosophy at the time of the interview, not sure of what she believed. She had read about that type of process in A Course in Miracles which gave her hope that she will flow forward again.

Native American Indian ritual dancing has helped unblock the flow of her intuition. At the ritual, each person performs an impromptu dance based on what they want to express or heal about themselves. When it was Paula's turn, she observed that her body moved on its own while her mind interpreted the movements. She experienced her body telling the story of creation through its movements. She has learned to be aware of her body and listen to the understanding or intuition that follows.

The dance group took a spiritual walk a few months before the interview to observe nature and share insights with each other. Paula's insight disturbed her. She felt that the only meaning in life was experiencing the present moment. Spiritual goals, enlightenment, and looking to the future seemed meaningless. With that perspective, she said it didn't matter if she had one or a hundred more lifetimes. She no longer felt the pressure of reaching some spiritual goal. *"In some ways, I think I'm closer to the truth by saying 'Hey, it doesn't matter,' than searching for directions."* She said that insight prompted the ebbing process that she was experiencing at the time of the interview.

Paula's spiritual pursuits are the most important thing in her life. She sees spirituality not as a destination, but a journey to enjoy and live with enthusiasm. She looks forward to moving out of her current confusion back to a clearer sense of her relationship with God and where she is heading.

Spiritual Beliefs

Paula has always lived with a respect for life that she learned from her parents. She believes there is order and a greater intelligence in the universe. Her increased trust in the universe and herself has eliminated her fear of death. She said she is happier and more peaceful than she was at twenty-five. She wonders sometimes how much of her insight and new strength is related to New Age versus the results of having children and just getting older and more mellow. She imagines the real test of her beliefs will come in thirty or forty years when she faces old age.

As to the purpose of life, Paula said people are here to grow and evolve, but also just to live in tune with the life source-God. *"A 'bad' life may not always be karmically caused. It may be just a side trip we chose to experience."* She said confusion about one's life can help bypass blocks in the rational mind, allowing truth to sneak in through the cracks.

Paula thinks the earth may move in cycles of closeness to God or spirituality. The earth may be coming out of a winter cycle in which materialism has flourished. The summer cycle may bring the planet a greater awareness of God and who we are.

When Paula came to believe in God, she saw him as a higher human partner, a being she could talk to, pray to, and ask for guidance. Before entering the "ebbing" state, she always felt God at her side and gave Him her problems. The only way she could feel a relationship with God was to feel a oneness with all that is. She had a glimpse of that relationship, but wasn't living it all the time. At the time of the interview, she felt a separation from God and was depending on herself.

Growth Techniques

Reading has been the most important technique for Paula. She has also benefitted from past-life regressions, yoga, Tai Chi, and music.

While she is not a "joiner," she enjoys a network of friends with whom she can exchange books, ideas, and experiences.

A psychic told her about food allergies she had. When she stopped eating those foods, she felt relaxed, lost weight, and had more energy and stamina.

She uses obstacles in her life to motivate her to do more, be better, and try different things.

Update (August 1989)

In the spring of 1989, Paula moved out of her spiritually ebbing state to one of more balance. Instead of searching outside for the Source or God, she focused on feeling it in all of creation around her. She doesn't feel separated from God any longer. She focuses on being fully present with herself and other people. *"I am now moving into an action oriented phase in my life. The six years of inner focus brought me strength, confidence, vision, and intuitive talents....I'm a spiritual teacher to myself. I have my own visions and inner direction....I'm a visionary dedicated to helping in this time on earth and being part of ushering in a New Age on earth."*

Russell (36, United Church of Christ background, geophysicist)

Russell (real name) had a happy childhood in New York, went to college, and enjoys a high paying career as a geophysicist. His spiritual awakening came after he underwent rolfing sessions to realign his body. That led to a spiritual correspondence course and later to a lead role in a spiritual center.

Life Experiences

Russell spent a happy childhood in New York. He went to the Unitarian church and later the United Church of Christ with his parents. He recalls his mother had metaphysical interests, but Russell wasn't interested as a child.

After graduating from college, Russell started work as a geophysicist, making a good salary so that he could do or buy whatever he wanted. He rarely thought about spiritual matters, although he went to an occasional workshop.

In early 1981, Russell started a series of rolfing[6] sessions consisting of deep tissue and muscle work designed to put the body back into alignment. He said he felt drawn to it without knowing what the purpose or consequences would be since he didn't have a particular physical problem he wanted to work on. Russell said rolfing treatments often open up the emotional, mental, and spiritual selves by allowing energy to flow more freely. He felt his spiritual energy channels open, clearing the way for his new interest in spiritual growth.

First, Russell began to question his religious beliefs. If something new fit his spiritual concept of God, he kept it. *"It was helpful to grow up in a religious atmosphere where I was exposed to several different churches. If I hadn't had that background, I might not have questioned it later."* He believes that many young people don't find traditional religion appealing because of its regimentation, following rules without knowing why. *"There are so many different beliefs. Who is right? Christianity is a minority in terms of the world religions. How can a Christian believe that if he's right, then seventy-five percent of the world is wrong and won't be saved? Does that sound like a principle God wants me to believe, a principle that Jesus Christ would profess?"*

Russell makes a distinction between religion and spirituality. *"Religion is following one set of beliefs, one person, one sect, one doctrine of faith, one something. Spirituality is a way of life, something I follow twenty-four hours a day."*

Russell started a correspondence course in 1981 which involved studying Alice Bailey's[7] works. The scientific nature of her writings

---

6. Rolfing. A series of bodywork sessions which aim for structural alignment and balance through deep tissue manipulation. The process was founded by Ida P. Rolf.
7. Alice Bailey was a member of the Theosophical Society and later started the Arcane School for spiritual study. From 1920 to her death in 1949, she channeled several books from a member of the spiritual hierarchy named Djwahl Khul or "the Tibetan."

appealed to his mind, and he spent five years working with the course-reading, answering questions, and meditating four times a day.

After a year of rolfing and correspondence work, Russell found a local spiritual center, the Creative Light Center, and began going to its classes and church services. The weekly classes, correspondence course, and church sessions gave him satisfaction and fullness he hadn't felt before. Everything in his life gained more meaning.

His full-time job was going well, but Russell began to feel guilty that he was so fortunate. Later, he realized that it isn't how much money you have or how you earn it that counts, but rather what you do with it and what your motives are. He saw that his talents included making money. His interest in spirituality grew as he looked at what he did with his money. He decided to share his money and show others how they can get their financial and business life in order and make it fulfilling for them. He said the principles came easily to him from reading Alice Bailey's works. *"You can have the right motives and principles and still be successful in the everyday world. The most spiritual way I can live is to live in society with the everyday problems, with a good job, keeping balanced, and never compromising my principles."*

After a year, the center's founder asked Russell to become an ordained counselor because of his contributions to the center. He agreed, and a year later he filled an opening on the board of directors. His involvement grew as he became a minister and later a vice president of the corporation that ran the center. When the founder decided to take a sabbatical, Russell took over as the state director to keep the center open. The first six months of 1987 were hectic for Russell, holding his full-time job and working every spare hour keeping the center running. The founder awarded him a Doctorate of Divinity for his work.

Russell's center encourages growth through group work. He prefers a variety of backgrounds and beliefs so that members can learn from each other. People who don't have open minds or aren't benefitting will stop coming to meetings. Through a natural process, a cohesive group forms without making rules or actively controlling membership.

Russell said there are some lessons, messages, and energies that can only be experienced in groups. The groups learn as the members work together. The lessons apply to the daily life of work, family, and relationships. In the work environment, the group mind will emerge rather than individuals giving orders. Since more people have input, Russell believes that businesses will run more smoothly, efficiently, and productively. That is the energy he sees awakening in the Aquarian age. He tries to model it by listening to others, rather than forcing his ideas on them.

Russell's full-time job and devotion to running the spiritual center had him in a state of exhaustion by the time of the interview. He hadn't taken a vacation purely for relaxation since he graduated from college fourteen years earlier. He was taking his first one the week after the interview. He admitted to being a workaholic, but wanted to get his life into better balance. *"You can't work at anything twenty-four hours a day, not even spirituality."*

Spiritual Beliefs

Russell tries to set an example by doing rather than preaching. He tries not to judge or criticize others. He sees each person as a manifestation of God and looks at them with the principles of harmlessness (from Alice Bailey's works) no matter what they have done.

Russell sees life as a learning process in which layers are peeled off in an effort to get to the core-the true self. Life's lessons involve physical healing, past traumas, repressed emotions, and societal pressures. As soon as one problem is solved, another comes along. *"We are all working on the same problems in different ways. There will be good times on top of the mountain and bad times in the valley, but they are all just something to experience. There is no shortcut to spirituality. You have to go through the pain for the growth and the lesson."*

Anything that embodies the principles of harmlessness and true spiritual love is God, according to Russell. *"God can be as mundane or simple as a flower, open to all to see no matter what race you are, how rich you are, or where you are going. God is an entity or force to guide us, instruct us, give us pleasure, and help us grow. There are different ways to God, and I'm following my way."*

Growth Techniques

Group work helps Russell work through obstacles. The best therapy for him is to talk to other people with similar problems for insights into how they handle them. They do that in small groups at his spiritual center. *"A lot of people can't discuss problems with their family so they need other people of like beliefs who aren't judgmental."*

Russell said that group work is an important aspect of the Aquarian age. The previous age, the Piscean age, was about individual accomplishment, with teacher and students separated. He said that certain levels of growth can happen in groups that can't happen individually.

He recommends that new searchers expose themselves to different groups and authors. *"Spend six months, a year, or years doing that and find out what beliefs you feel most comfortable with and then follow them. Traditional religion may be your path, or there are free groups or groups that run on donations. But don't do something because someone else found enlightenment doing it, do it for yourself. And you should still keep an open mind because your beliefs will most likely continue to change."*

Update (August 1989)

When Russell came back from his vacation in the fall of 1988, he found that his company planned to consolidate his regional office into one in another state. He had to decide whether to wait for a transfer or a layoff notice or to accept the severance package. He said the time he took off to recover his health helped clear his mind, and he decided to give up the security of his job and follow the spiritual pull of his heart to stay where he was.

At first, he looked for similar jobs and even considered going back to college, but his heart wasn't in it. When he asked himself what he wanted to do, the answer was to run the Creative Light Center full-time. He didn't know how he would do it, but he wanted to try. He was working to revise the board of directors and increase membership so that donations and class fees would support the center. Next, he wanted to look for a part-time job to cover his own bills. *"As of right now, I have two months of living expenses left, but I am determined to see this through. If it's time for an Aquarian group to be successful, I would like to be a part of it now."*

Sydney (45, atheistic background, teacher)

Sydney (real name) is a wife, mother, and teacher who found God after twenty-seven years as a self-proclaimed atheist. She never thought about spiritual matters until curiosity about the brain's potential opened the door for her.

Life Experiences

Sydney had no religious training as a child. When Sydney was six, her grandmother gave her a book of Bible stories. *"After reading them, I thought that if God knew whether I was going to be good or bad even before I was born, why even bother. It didn't make sense to me. I was told to have faith, but I didn't know how to get it."*

In college, Sydney asked the chaplain why every discipline except religion told her to use her mind. She didn't get an answer. *"One day in the dormitory when no one was around, I said, 'I don't believe in God.' I waited to see if a lightning bolt would strike me down. When nothing happened, I decided life had no purpose.*" She was afraid she could die any day and then there would be nothing. She feared that people and things she loved would be taken away. So she decided to live for the fun of the moment since the future seemed out of her control.

Sydney eventually married and had children, which prompted her to wonder about God again. *"I knew that no matter what the children did wrong, I would never send them to burn in hell. And I couldn't imagine a God that would."* So she reaffirmed that God didn't exist. She believed that people invented God because death frightened them.

In early 1988, information about the brain's potential sparked Sydney's curiosity as a teacher. She started reading about the mind and visualization as a means to make things happen. One book she particularly liked was *Heading Toward Omega* by Kenneth Ring, a book about near-death experiences (NDE). Sydney felt a kinship with the thoughts and experiences reported by those people, even though she had not had a NDE.

Later, she felt guided to a spiritual teacher who talked to her about astral projection and introduced her to the teachings of Ramtha[8]. Sydney says that Ramtha's book is her bible. Several of Ramtha's video tapes confirmed long-held feelings and helped open her to new ideas. She learned to listen to her inner voice as a guide to perceiving reality. Sydney agrees with Ramtha's teaching that "becoming is an alone process." Since Sydney's focus has changed so drastically in her life, she finds there are only a few people she can talk to about her transformation. Now that her spiritual growth is the most important thing in her life, she has dropped friendships that were based on superficial activities, such as shopping and having lunch.

Sydney said her new beliefs have improved her relationship with her son. He had been self-destructive after Sydney divorced his father, and psychiatrists told her that her son was doing as well as could be expected. But as she changed by following Ramtha's teaching "to just allow people to be," she said her son became a joy. When she stopped trying to control him and acknowledged his feelings, his temper tantrums stopped.

To improve all of her relationships, Sydney tries to give up the need to be right and to control. She has learned to let emotions pass through her rather than letting them control her. When she realizes her emotions are in charge, she works to put everything back into proper perspective. And she tries to forgive herself when she falls back into her old habits because she finds guilt destructive to her progress.

---

8. Ramtha is an entity who channels through the body of JZ Knight.

Sydney's second husband, raised a strict Southern Baptist, is open to her beliefs and attends workshops with her. Her beliefs are such an important part of her life that she doesn't try to cover it up from friends or relatives who don't understand.

Her beliefs have also influenced her teaching. She talks to her students about happiness, honesty, and other New Age concepts, leaving out the religious or spiritual specifics. She once asked them to write a paper on the topic, "Unhappiness in Life is Inevitable-True or False." *"I was amazed when they all said it was true. I pointed out how limiting that view was and that they were defeating themselves from the start."*

Her beliefs also help defuse situations that used to anger her. *"When students act up, I see it as a learning experience for me rather than thinking that they're trying to cause me problems. Seeing life as lessons has taken so much anger out of me."*

Sydney cites another example related to traffic problems. *"I look at faces and see so many that look tired and defeated. Once, when I let a couple of cars into traffic, the woman behind me started honking and shaking her fist at me. I thought how unhappy she must be when my doing something nice for someone else made her so angry. In the old days, I would have wanted to jump out of my car and stomp her into the ditch."*

Sydney tries to accept that she can't help other people unless they ask for it. But seeing people in pain or anger troubles her since she has found a way out for herself.

Maintaining a sense of detachment, which she studied in A Course in Miracles, also challenges her. At the time of the interview, Sydney had a dying aunt. She felt prepared for her aunt's death because she knew her aunt would be fine after her body died. She says she still has work to do on maintaining that same sense of detachment related to her children. Since the interview, Sydney wrote that her aunt died. *"I had a few teary moments, but handled it well. I realized my tears are for me, not her. She's fine!"*

Spiritual Beliefs

Sydney believes that God made everything out of Himself. *"Separateness of beings and living things is an illusion. Everyone can know God if they can get rid of that illusion."* Entering heaven or hell after only one lifetime never made sense to her. She discovers her own spiritual truth by thinking first and sensing the thoughts transforming into a feeling of knowing. She believes that losing her anger and irritation and being a happier and kinder person indicate that she is on a "good and right" path for her.

The purpose of life, she believes, is to learn and experience. She recently realized that she likes to judge people. Becoming aware of that allowed her to decide to change that behavior. She says awareness is the key to learning. She quotes Ramtha again, *"You can't see something in someone else unless it is in you."* Now when people or situations disturb her, she looks for the aspect of herself that is calling for change.

Growth Techniques

Books and tapes have had the strongest influence on her. The books include *Heading Toward Omega* by Kenneth Ring, *Beyond Super Nature* by Lyall Watson, and the Lazaris, Ramtha, and Seth materials.[9] She also worked with a spiritual teacher for a time.

Sydney uses visualization regularly and keeps a journal to get clear about the changes she wants in herself and her life. She also has used visualization techniques to heal herself and her daughter of minor ailments. She said she knows how to be happy every moment and how to create her dreams. *"That doesn't mean I can do it all now, but I know what I have to do to get there."*

When she feels impatient about her growth, she looks back at how much she has changed in the prior six months. She says that God has developed a *"wonderful, fail-safe system of spiritual growth. You can't tell someone else about it. They have to discover it for themselves. To get the power that is available, you have to get rid of the negative aspects of yourself. So when you get the power, you have the wisdom to use it the way God planned."*

Update (May 1989)

Since the interview, Sydney wrote a letter saying that she had been trying to "manifest" major changes in her life for a year. The changes included moving to the mountains, working at home, and learning about organic gardening and nutrition in addition to devoting more time to metaphysics. She started visualizing her desired results without planning how to accomplish them. After a year, money came to her unexpectedly, and she and her family are moving to a city in the mountains where they plan to build a solar house. She ended the letter, *"This whole thing is TRUE! Isn't it grand. I never knew I could be so happy!"*

---

9. Lazaris,Ramtha and Seth are all channeled entities whose teachings can be found in the form of books and audio and video tapes.

Your life works best when you love, serve, and flow your loving energy-not from a lower consciousness motivation of "I am helping you," or "I will save you," but simply from the awareness that "the universe gave this energy to me and it feels good to pass it along."

- Handbook to Higher Consciousness

7   Always Spiritually Aware

Each of these people had unusual spiritual or psychic experiences as a child. Most were not believed when they tried to tell others about the experiences, and many began to deny them even to themselves. This often led to a denial of their spiritual side until adulthood. But the spiritual experience was always with them, and eventually they came face to face with their spiritual beliefs again.

Catherine (36, Lutheran background, spiritual counselor)

Catherine's (real name) parents and brother battered her as a child. She found no support for loving herself from her family or church. She ignored her interests in writing and music to prove herself in the corporate world. After years of success in her work, she realized it gave her no pleasure and that she was as far from her soul as she had ever been. Counseling and channeling helped her get control of her life, and she found the inner resources and guidance to discover the spiritual child she had left behind many years before.

Life Story

Catherine came from a dysfunctional family in which the dysfunction was battering. As a child, she and her older brother protected each other until he learned from his father that men batter, and he started beating her too. *"That was a great sense of loss for me because my companion was gone. I had to have a lock on my bedroom door so my brother and father couldn't beat me. Then my mother became a batterer."*

With all the pain in her life, Catherine was confused by the sense of fullness she felt in her heart when she would lie in bed. It contradicted everything that was happening to her. Her parents called her Cathy, but the feeling of fullness always came with her full name, Catherine. She sensed people without bodies talking to her at night. *"They would say, 'You are not the way people are treating you; don't get mixed up; don't get confused. You are loved. You are important. You are special.'"* Then she could go to sleep. But she would wake up confused again by the contradictions in her outer life. She wouldn't tell anyone about the voices because they would think she was crazy. *"I thought the voice was Jesus because I heard in church that Jesus loved the little children."* She said the voices never told her what to do; they just gave her an overwhelming sense of love.

The pressure to be like everyone else forced her to close off her experiences with the voices. She remembered a friend talking about her own unseen companion. Catherine was conscious of being tender with her friend, but she wasn't going to talk about her own voices because she began to lose confidence that she actually heard them. She wouldn't allow that vulnerability anymore.

At thirteen, when she was introduced to the pastor at church, Catherine saw what he was thinking moving across his forehead like words on an electronic billboard. She said his actions didn't agree with his thoughts. She got support from her mother for this experience because her mother had had some unusual experiences.

The pastor told Catherine that Jesus would look for stray sheep for only a certain amount of time before going back to the rest of the flock. She thought he was implying that she was a stray sheep because she questioned his authority to tell her how to live her personal life. Since she wasn't allowed to interpret Christianity from her own special place, she tried other religions. They all told her to be a certain way so that people would approve of her. But no one told her how to love herself, which is what she needed to do. Loving Jesus so that He would love her wasn't enough.

By high school, Catherine was looking to others to tell her who she was. *"I got lost in the competition, accomplishment, and labeling that is so much a part of our society."* While Catherine secretly thought of herself as a writer and musician, she decided to prove herself in the corporate world after high school. She got mixed signals at work regarding using her intuition versus logic. Two mentors advised her to trust her intuition because it was often right. Other people wanted her to be more mechanical or mental about her work. She used both successfully and found herself promoted several times.

Catherine noticed that she got more rewards and credibility from using logic and reason. So she moved further away from her true self. The company increased its expectations of her. Their demands and her pushing herself started taking its toll. *"Before I knew it, all the joy was gone. Everything I thought I knew about myself was gone. My dream to make enough money to quit to be a writer disappeared. I focused on the next promotion, how I would get through the week, and why the weekend was so short."*

The question, "Is this all there is?" started to go through her mind. "What am I going to be like when I'm forty?" Her colleagues in their late 20's talked about being with the company until retirement, a thought that appalled her. Just enough of her inner voice remained for her to hear, "Be true to yourself." But she didn't know what that meant anymore. Occasionally, one of her mentors would come to her and say, "You're really good at writing, what are you doing here?"

Catherine became very ill and was in continuous pain, leading to addiction to pain pills. She finally admitted to herself that her life was out of control. She made a list of all the things wrong with her body-eyesight problems, ringing in her ears, pain in her head and back, and dragging one leg. And she drank and used drugs. Seeing how sick she was scared her. Doctors told her her condition was common for a woman in a high tension job, and they prescribed relaxation. But she was so afraid to go inside herself and relax that she sought counseling.

Then Catherine took a business trip to Hawaii and sat on a beach thinking about what a wreck her life was. And intuitively, she knew it was her fault. A song went through her head about making it home again. *"Then I remembered going to a psychic at sixteen who told me I would be sitting somewhere and would hear a song about home. I realized there was a home, and I needed to get there."*

As she had made a list of her physical ailments, she made a list of her spiritual ills. *"I literally had to go to the dictionary to look 'spiritual' up. I had lost all sense of it."* She had just enough spark left to feel confident she could find her spiritual home. She continued her counseling, made changes at work, started saying "No," and asked for changes from her dysfunctional family.

When she tried to change her role at work while management changes were going on, her company fired her. *"That was great. I woke up the next day saying, 'Wonderful. I get to do anything I want with my life, and I'm really scared about it. But I would rather die than live the way I've been living.'"*

Catherine started reading about dysfunctional families and metaphysical topics. She married during this time and started work as a business writer then as a personal growth writer.

After going to a channeling session with her husband, Catherine learned to channel, and the feelings of fullness, love, and never being alone came rushing back. The majority of her growth came from channeling. She developed a relationship with her spiritual teachers that allowed her to go inside and get specific instructions on how to recognize limiting thoughts and move beyond them.

For two years, Catherine apprenticed by working with other channels. Then for nine months, she quit writing and working outside and spent each day channeling or doing exercises related to channeling. Her spiritual guides gave her information about herself and always asked if she wanted more, never forcing anything on her. After that period, she went to three different channeled spiritual teachers who each said she was ready to channel for others.

Catherine has a partnership with her teachers. They let her know when she clouds her counseling with her own issues so she can back off. She said there are times when nothing comes through for people, and she tells them that rather than making up something. She doesn't think of her teachers as higher but as unlimited. She evaluates what they say against criteria she has developed. Is there a sense of love, humility, and oneness? Do they empower people by showing them that the answer is within them? Do they encourage growth? Her teachers never give specific answers because that limits the recipient, and the answer would change as the person changes.

As Catherine has worked on healing herself, she has been rejected by her family, which she said is common when people try to change a dysfunctional system. She hasn't seen her family for six years by their choice, not hers.

A major challenge for Catherine and her husband is changing the present without planning for the future, "the ultimate letting go of control." They were wondering if they should move at the time of the interview. Catherine said they had stopped setting external goals. They just try to be who they are and experience it. She knows that decisions to change will come from within at the right time.

Life Goals

Catherine seeks only to be present in each moment, resisting pulls from the past or future. Her inner goals are to be aware of limiting beliefs and to move through them. Because of her perspective on life, she tries to be creative in adapting her new self to an outside world that has different assumptions about people, their motives, and how things should be done.

Spiritual Beliefs

Catherine said she lost control of her life, but in a positive way. *"I don't have to control my life anymore, and I don't have to control other people's lives. I don't expect people to be a certain way and can accept and love them as they are."*

She believes that whatever is right for her is right for the other people she is involved with. She described three phases of being a human being: totally self-centered motivated by inner "shoulds," "we" consciousness driven by outside "shoulds," and the lack of ego or just experiencing with no "shoulds."

When Catherine got new glasses at age five, she stood underneath a tree looking at the bees in the blooms. She had just learned in Sunday school that God had created everything, but she wondered who created God. And she still looks for that ultimate Source. As soon as she gets a sense of God, she looks behind that. She doesn't see God as one omnipotent being or as a nameless, faceless energy. Her sense of God is personal, intimate, and fun. She feels that each person is an extension of the Source, reporting back his experiences.

Her teachers are there because they like supporting and aiding other beings. Catherine doesn't have a sense of a greater game plan. She said all beings are going to return to the Source sharing their consciousness with it no matter what path they take. She and her teachers are going home in their unique ways.

Catherine doesn't ask about what the future will bring. Other channels have warned of coming drastic physical changes to the earth and have advised people to prepare. *"You can be attached to the physical body and planet or remember that you are movement, change, energy, and growth. Some entities may be trying to get people to understand the coming changes so they won't be afraid, but it produces fear. People should learn instead to be detached about whatever happens and be in the moment."*

Growth Techniques

While channeling has been the greatest force in her growth, Catherine relied on reading for additional insights and tools. First, she read books related to setting up a business and being prosperous. Then she moved to books about visualization, which led her to trust her invisible side. After reading a book about free-lance writing that said a writer should be honest with herself, she started keeping a journal.

Catherine spent some time in support groups, but decided to stop going so that she wasn't continually getting information from outside herself. She misses the groups because she learned a lot listening to other people. But she hasn't found a new group she feels comfortable with. She sees herself on a lonely part of her path. But to keep from becoming a hermit, she creates opportunities to get out and is considering joining some writers' groups again.

Carol (47, Baptist background, radio advertising)

Carol grew up in a strict Baptist household. She escaped her mother's abuse by marrying before finishing high school. Her second marriage to an alcoholic resulted in a mental breakdown. After she divorced and regained her strength, she found a metaphysical community that provided her with tools to recover her confidence and self-worth.

Life Story

When Carol was five, an elderly cousin to whom she was close appeared at the end of Carol's bed and told her good-bye. Soon after, Carol's parents received a call telling them the cousin had died. *"When I found out she had died, I thought there had to be a life after death. I told my sister what happened, but not my parents. One of my sisters said our dead grandmother used to come and wrap her up at night, especially if her feet were sticking out. My sister dreaded it and pleaded with grandmother not to come."* But Carol soon put thoughts of life after death out of her mind.

Carol's mother came from a very strict Baptist background and raised her children the same way. In the beginning, Carol learned not to question the church's teachings. As she got older, however, she noticed questions in her father's mind. *"He was very quiet and seldom shared his spiritual thoughts with me. But I did hear him ask questions, and he had New Age type books lying around, and I had an older married sister who had investigated other spiritual beliefs. I remember thinking that lightning hadn't struck them dead, so I thought it was OK to question some of the things I had been taught."*

As a teenager, Carol was confused and rebellious in thought, if not in action. *"I knew my mother would kill me if I did some of the things I thought about. I was scared to death of her. She would smack first and ask questions later."*

Carol's father died when she was fifteen. She was a poor student and very shy until she discovered boys. *"During that period, I needed approval, understanding, and affection. I used to think about throwing myself in front of a car. I thought then people would miss me."*

Carol's first rebellious act was to marry while in high school and then drop out. She had a daughter at eighteen, but her marriage lasted only a year. *"We couldn't live together. We had done a stupid thing as children. He had a bad family life too that he was trying to escape."*

After her divorce, Carol made some money playing piano to support herself and her daughter. *"I was totally confused about what to do. I looked for spiritual truth through reading. I met some people who had known Edgar Cayce. One woman was so calm and at peace with herself that I thought there had to be something to that. So I read a lot of Cayce information, and I never stopped believing in God. Even though I didn't have a lot of answers, my spiritual beliefs got stronger and started calming me down."*

At twenty-five, Carol married again to a man who had no interest in her spiritual beliefs. But she continued to study and learned about astrology from one of her sisters. *"The more I read and did, the more I loved it. I couldn't stop. I have tried and given up a lot of other things, but astrology has been an on-going passion for me."*

Carol's husband was an alcoholic, and her marriage was very unhappy. *"If it hadn't been for my beliefs, my interest in astrology, and looking for a light in those bad times, I probably wouldn't be here today. I was very depressed at the time."*

Her astrology chart gave her hope when she saw a favorable time for ending her marriage. But she struggled with the prospect of a second failed marriage. She thought something was wrong with her. *"One day when my husband had been drinking, he broke a mahogany coffee table that my father had made. I was so angry that I grabbed a hammer and wanted to hit him in the head. But I thought, 'Now wait, you don't want to go to jail and never see your children again. You don't want to take somebody else's life.' I broke down from the stress and ended up in the hospital."*

When Carol was released from the hospital, she still felt half dead. She asked for a divorce after twelve years in that marriage. She was so drained that it took about three years to get her health back. *"I took a job in a shirt factory because I didn't have the mental energy at the time to deal with people or to make decisions. My back killed me. I punched in and out and had to ask permission to go to the bathroom. But I'm glad I did it, it taught me humility."*

When she got stronger, Carol decided to devote time to herself. She moved to a nearby city and went to a more open church. She began selling radio advertising, which she had done with her ex-husband. *"I didn't finish high school, but one thing I can do is sell."*

Carol discovered the local metaphysical and holistic community. She met a Tarot reader who told her more about herself than her astrology charts did. *"I felt like I had found my people."* Carol continued searching and was often rewarded by meeting the right person or finding the right book at the right time.

Astrology and Tarot taught Carol to trust her own intuition and judgement. The accuracy of her readings for herself and a few others have given her the confidence to give readings for more people without judging or screening the information she receives.

Carol's mother became ill, and she lived with Carol and her daughter for about a year and a half before she died. Even while she was ill, she tried to run Carol's and her granddaughter's lives. She had stroke after stroke and couldn't be left alone. Carol had little life of her own during that time. *"After she died, I prayed for a long time because I felt that she still hadn't let go of her life here. I had dreams that she was still clinging to this life. I tried to tell her to let go, that she had things to do. The dreams stopped about a year and a half after she died."*

Carol is glad for the time she spent with her mother because she thinks she learned to understand her. *"It finally sunk in to me that she was just a product of how she was raised. She did the best she could with her life and with the knowledge she had. I needed to know that, and I don't think I could have learned that without her staying with me."*

After her mother's death, Carol decided to slow down her life. *"My work was too cut throat, and I felt that I was getting an ulcer. Everything was too expensive for me. It was a steady fight just to keep the lights turned on."*

Carol moved to a small town nearer her sisters. She enjoys her job selling radio ads there and has one friend with whom she can discuss her spiritual beliefs. Otherwise she keeps them to herself since there is no metaphysical community there.

Carol's older daughter shares some of her spiritual beliefs. Carol did past-life readings for her daughter to give her insights that helped resolve some marriage problems. A friend introduced Carol's younger daughter to the Baptist church. *"Anything they don't understand is the work of the devil. Now my daughter thinks what I do is the devil's work. She tried to argue her beliefs with me, and we finally had to come to a truce and not discuss each other's beliefs."*

Life Goals

Carol doesn't describe herself as career-oriented nor does she set goals, which frustrates her bosses. She does as much as she can each day, and she hopes for a successful personal relationship. *"For a long time, I didn't want to date anybody or live through another painful relationship. I had enough interests to entertain myself for years. But after being on my own for ten years, I'm ready to share the rest of my life with a compatible mate. Sometimes I just want to touch somebody. I'm thankful my family and friends like to touch and hug."*

Carol also hopes to overcome the lack of money in her life, and she has a group of friends with the same problem. She uses affirmations and visualizations to try to attract money.

Spiritual Beliefs

"My close friends would probably say I am not very spiritual because they don't hear me talk about it. But they don't know what I feel inside. My spiritual beliefs made me a new person after my divorce. I learned I could depend on myself for food, clothing, and shelter. I developed confidence and a self of self-worth."

Carol tries to integrate her spiritual beliefs in her daily life by doing more than her job requires and by not selling someone something they don't need. *"Just yesterday, I cut someone's advertising budget in half because I didn't think they needed that big a budget."*

Carol's concept of God is a wonderful understanding person with "one heck of a sense of humor."

Growth Techniques

Carol has used astrology and Tarot cards to help her make decisions. A hypnotist has helped her to explore past lives. She also values prayer. *"The most spiritual thing to me is going to the beach when no one else is around and just sitting there. It releases all my tension. I do it as often as I can to survive."*

"The advice I give myself everyday is to stop taking everything so seriously. I tend to be the family worrier. God gave us a sense of humor, and people should use it to ease the tensions in their life."

Ted (41, Methodist background, owns a recording studio)

Ted had a spiritual experience as a child, but turned his back on religion after high school. In college, Ted used drugs in his search for God. Trying to provide a spiritual base for his children brought him back to the church where he served as a lay Methodist minister until he realized he didn't believe what he preached. Then one of Shirley MacLaine's books put him back on his spiritual path.

Life Story

As a pre-teen at a day camp, Ted said he had a spiritual experience while watching a burning cross used in one of the camp programs. It signalled to him that he needed to pay attention to spiritual things and that there were things bigger than himself.

Ted stopped going to the Methodist church after high school because he had a conflict with the teachings and the way they were presented. He resented having the teachings forced on him without being encouraged to develop his own understanding of them.

In college, Ted tried mind-altering drugs in his search for answers. After graduating with a degree in broadcasting, he went away for a few weeks to decide what to do next. When he returned, he found a draft notice in his mail box. That night, he took LSD and felt he had a mystical experience. *"I had a vision of a ball of clay with a big finger over it. A drop of green fell from it to the clay, and life began. That was all I needed to believe in God."* Ted assumed he had experienced a Christian rebirth and went back to church, but he didn't stay when he discovered that spirituality and religion weren't necessarily the same.

After his military commitment, Ted married and started a career in radio broadcasting. After ten years of marriage and two children, he renewed his interest in the metaphysical. He took a Silva Mind Control course which led to psychic experiences. But his wife didn't share his interests, and they soon divorced.

Finding less pleasure in his radio work, Ted tried other ways to make money, such as painting and selling office supplies. He tried radio once more, but he was so miserable that he left again. He eventually set up his own recording studio and turned it into a successful business.

Then Ted married a woman with children, and they had more of their own. Wanting to introduce his children to spiritual teaching, he tried the Methodist church again. His growing involvement led to his becoming a certified lay minister, Sunday school teacher, and liturgist. *"But I had trouble grappling with certain teachings, such as Jesus Christ being the only son of God. I realized I was saying things in front of the church that I didn't believe, and I was torn over it."*

After Ted read *Dancing in the Light* by Shirley MacLaine, he realized his spiritual life was incomplete. A few months later, he told his minister he was taking a leave of absence and probably wouldn't return.

Ted began investigating New Age thinking, and answers began falling into place. He learned that all the answers were inside him, and he just had to be quiet and listen for them. *"I felt that spirituality was a personal thing, a way of living, and that religion tried to impose that from the outside. To me, religion is a system of beliefs and spirituality is the practice of what you believe."*

Ted struggled to explain his reason for leaving the church to his father, who was a son of a Methodist minister. *"I told him that religion gives you a closed box with everything you need to know inside. I had been in the box, but the top kept coming off. I kept seeing things the church couldn't explain, and*

I decided that religion led to a dead end while spirituality was open-ended. I wanted to continue to learn about myself, nature, and God and to come closer to the best I could be."

Ted completed a course called Technologies for Creating which helped him put his spiritual beliefs into practice. The course taught him there aren't any obstacles, just opportunities. He learned practical tools to create what he wants. He also learned to control his moods. *"A problem arose with someone, and my first reaction was that it was going to be a hassle. But I stopped and said it didn't have to be. I backed off, cleared my mind, and said this can be cleared up easily. I chose for it not to be an obstacle, and it no longer was."*

Ted said that visualization helped him sell his house in three weeks for the price he wanted. He said he pictured the current and desired realities. While looking for a new house, he and his wife made a list of what they wanted and continually revised it. Ted drew a sketch of the land and a floor plan for the house they hoped to find, and he continued to visualize it. They could hardly believe it when they found a house and land just like their drawings. But they did believe it, and they bought it.

Regarding business, Ted plans to develop skills and interests beyond his recording studio which will allow him to be more personally creative. Becoming a stronger communicator and using more than his voice is part of that plan.

Spiritual Beliefs

Ted said he feels at odds with organized religion. He believes that Jesus was misquoted when his words were written down and that the church misinterpreted the Bible in its attempt to teach it. *"Anything touched by man,"* Ted said, *"is bound to lose some of its purity."*

Ted likes the teachings of the Unity church. Although he and his family don't go often, he says it is a place to worship God while believing what you want. Ted agrees that Jesus was a profound teacher. *"I think one of the most important things Jesus said was his response to his disciples' amazement at the miracles he performed. He asked why they were amazed since they could do the same and more. But traditional religion has ignored that. We can accomplish miracles every day through the power of our mind, intellect, and spirit."*

Ted sees God as energy or white light to which each person connects. He believes we created this universe with God and chose to experience life on this planet as physical beings.

Growth Techniques

Meditation, Silva Mind Control, the Technologies for Creating course, and prayer have been important activities in Ted's growth.

Books that were especially important to him were: Shirley MacLaine's *Out on a Limb, Dancing in the Light,* and *It's All in the Playing*; Levi's *The Aquarian Gospel of Jesus Christ* and *Jesus the Christ*; and Richard Bach's *Jonathan Livingston Seagull* and *Illusions*.

Rebecca (54, Catholic background, pharmacist)

Rebecca grew up with an insatiable curiosity and reluctance to take things on faith. This proved to alienate her from her family when she began looking for spiritual answers outside the Catholic religion. After two marriages that didn't work, she found herself drawn to metaphysical resources. After four years of esoteric spiritual studies, she learned to channel information that led to the discovery of her life's mission.

Life Story

Rebecca described her childhood as difficult and emotionally abusive, but she said it also helped strengthen her. In addition, her dream of learning to fly helped her struggle through the hard times. Her family didn't understand her urge to fly since no one else in the family flew. *"When I was seven years old, I built model airplanes. Other girls didn't do that. While I was at school, my mother would throw my airplanes away or hide them. But I'd just get them out again. Finally, when I was thirteen, my mother threw them in the trash one last time."* About that time, Rebecca told her parents she was going to pharmacy school, would make a lot of money, learn how to fly, and get an airplane. *"They didn't take me seriously, but whenever I say I'm going to do something, I do it."*

Rebecca went to Catholic schools until the tenth grade. She went to church every Sunday and to confession. But she grew up feeling different from everyone else. When she asked questions about religion, the nuns told her to have faith and believe. *"I sat there and thought, no, I can't. Something isn't right. I looked around the room and everyone else was happy accepting what she said. I interpreted that to mean that there was something wrong with me because I wasn't believing like all the others."*

As she got older, Rebecca continued going to church because her parents insisted. She enjoyed the music, the incense, and the ceremony, but didn't believe she would go to hell if she ate meat on Friday. *"They told* me that, and they scared me. As I got older, I felt that couldn't be right. God loves you and he's not going to do that to you. So I questioned and questioned."

Rebecca grew up without many friends. She sat in the corner reading all the time. She wanted to know why and how things worked. From age eight to fourteen, she read at least five books a day in the library. She studied most of the major religions. "I was searching, but I didn't know what I was looking for. I read what attracted me. I didn't understand that your soul guides you by being attracted to something. So all along I used to be hard on myself because I thought I was impulsive. I learned later that I had been following the right way all along."

By her twenties, Rebecca's parents weren't speaking with her. She never discussed her religious doubts with them. "I never felt that they liked me. My mother used to say to me, 'I hate you, you're no good, I wish I had never had you.'" So Rebecca kept searching, and when she felt strong enough, she left home and never went back to church.

Rebecca completed pharmacy school at twenty-two and used the money from her first job to take flying lessons. She couldn't afford an airplane, so she bought the pieces and built one herself. "I flew above the cumulus clouds in the summer, sang Strauss waltzes, and danced amid the clouds. It was wonderful. I experienced such joy in the air by myself. I had this draw for higher, for more. Now I see I was just trying to escape into the other dimensions. And I'm still trying to go higher and higher, looking for more."

She married a few years later to a man who also flew, so she spent twenty years flying. But she didn't pursue any spiritual interests during that time. "My husband wasn't interested, and I wasn't strong enough to go against what he wanted to do."

Having been on her own for a while, Rebecca wasn't comfortable with her husband's traditional view of men's and women's roles. But she felt powerless to do anything about it. She worked at the pharmacy part-time and then quit to be "the good housewife."

After a few years at home, she felt tired and depressed and could hardly move. She went to a doctor who told her the only thing wrong with her was boredom. "He told me to get some adventure in my life and to go back to work. I did, and I've been fine ever since. Trying to be other than true to myself was depressing."

Rebecca's husband agreed that she could go back to work, but expected her to drop everything to entertain his clients or go where he wanted to go. She didn't speak up for herself and found herself repressing her inner feelings. She finally knew the marriage had to end for her to survive, so she divorced him after nine years of marriage.

Two years later, Rebecca married again to a man who was more open to new ideas. She took the est[1] training and learned Transcendental Meditation. Her second marriage ended after seven years when she found herself working six days a week to support them and still being expected to do all the housework and cook the meals.

On July 4, 1977, Rebecca had a life changing experience. She was sitting at home reading a book when she heard a voice in her head say, *"Get in your car and look for property."* She put her book down, and thought she was imagining things. When she picked her book up to read again, the voice said the same thing. She had always criticized herself for her vivid imagination so she ignored it and tried to read again. This time the voice said, *"Look, it's a pretty day out, the sun is shining, you'll enjoy it. Go get in your car and look for property."*

Rebecca knew she wasn't going to be able to finish her book, so she went out and got in the car. *"I wasn't really disturbed. On some level I understood it. I got in my car and started driving around. I always knew that I wanted to live in the woods."* Rebecca was led to a wooded lot on a dead end street near other wooded areas, lakes, and meadows. When she saw the "for sale" sign on the property, she knew she was supposed to buy it. She signed papers to buy the property three days later.

For twenty years she had been collecting pictures of A-frame houses. Now she could build the house of her dreams. *"I had no idea there was any meaning to it. I felt like the man in 'Close Encounters of the Third Kind' who kept seeing this mountain he had to get to."* It took her four years to build the house after going through four lawyers and two builders.

A year before the house was completed, Rebecca noticed an advertisement for psychic power courses and decided to sign up. She began reading more books and wanted to take more classes. She started a four year program in a school of esoteric studies and went to classes at least two times a week. *"By the time I graduated, I was channeling information from spiritual guides and Ascended Masters."*

Then she decided to open her own school for metaphysical studies. She ran it part-time for a while and then quit her pharmacy job to work at it full-time. *"If anyone ever tells you getting on a spiritual path is easy and everything works out right, they're out of their mind. If I had known then what I was getting into, I say I wouldn't have done it. But knowing me, I probably would have anyway. I thought I could make a living doing readings and teaching classes. I had complete faith that I could do it because I had never failed at anything I had ever done. It never occurred to me that I would have any*

---

1. est is an abbreviation for Erhard Seminars Training, personal growth seminars that became popular in the late 1970's.

problems. But I had a big awakening coming. I took all my life savings and my IRA and quit work for two years to get everything started."

Not long after, Rebecca felt guided to buy a local metaphysical newspaper. She had five people in her classes at the time with newspaper experience. *"This is where I started learning about the difficulties when you get involved in this work because within two weeks I never saw any of them again. When you start doing serious work on your path that involves other people, sometimes their ego gets in the way, and they're not ready to do their soul's work, and off they go."*

Soon Rebecca found another woman who knew they were to work together. Then a few others joined the group. Most of them were able to channel and got the same information about what they were supposed to do as a group. Others felt drawn to the group, but many weren't able to commit to it. The group eventually added a bookstore to their projects.

After two years away from her job, Rebecca had the newspaper going, the school started, had found people who shared her vision, and was part owner of a bookstore. But she had run out of money and had to go back to work full-time. *"I did all this work to get things started and now that the fun has begun, I'm not there. I'm really having to work at not being angry about that. It doesn't seem fair. I knew that wasn't part of the plan, but people who were supposed to help didn't."*

The vision that Rebecca and the rest of her group hold is for a self-contained spiritual community. Most of the group has moved to the wooded areas near her. She said the plan hasn't worked out exactly as her guides had suggested. But she wonders whether her time frames and theirs are the same. *"When they say soon, I think next week, and they might mean five years from now."*

Rebecca says she gets information about the future in visions. *"It's like watching television. Pictures pop up the same as when I do past-life readings, and I just know their meaning."*

Her group gets confirmation of their information from other sources. *"Without that, it would be easy to think we were nuttier than a fruitcake. But other people like us also follow their guidance and have called us to tell us what they've received through channeling."*

Rebecca looks wistfully at her life before learning her spiritual mission. She enjoyed flying, dancing, and taking vacations. She has no time or money for that now. *"All I do is work at the pharmacy, work on the newspaper, and come home. It's like having six jobs. But I know what it's heading towards, so I keep going."*

For Rebecca, it's important to have people she can talk to about what she's doing to help keep her from thinking she's crazy. *"The New Age or Aquarian age is one of group work. We're meant to network and work with each other. There are people doing this everywhere; it's not as strange as people think. It's just that people are in the closet. They don't know that the people next door or down the street are doing the same things. They all think they're the only ones. If they would be more open with it, they would meet people like themselves."*

Rebecca is continually learning new things and looking for more. She is amazed by the information that she and the other members of her group channel. *"When I teach or write about something, I have to feel comfortable with it. If something doesn't seem right, we'll check it out with each other because we're getting new information all the time."* She and her group have found other groups across the country that are getting the same information they are. The information they receive is about building their spiritual community, about diets, changing bodily vibrations, the new energy coming to the earth, and major changes in the earth that are coming. *"I know I'm here as part of the large group of 'light workers' whose mission is to help humanity through the upcoming transition into the next dimension. It's similar to what the Bible's Book of Revelation refers to as the 'rapture.'"*

Rebecca's responsibility in the spiritual community is for the garden. She has felt pushed to learn ways to garden indoors, in containers, and using hydroponics in preparation for the earth changes. She said there are people throughout the country who are being guided to set up self-sufficient communities such as theirs. *"Some will find haven in a self-contained community. Others will not be drawn to that. It depends on your purpose. I wasn't worried about storing up food, and I was surprised when I got information about it. But I know we're supposed to be available to help others. After the transition, there have to be teachers all over the world who can tell humanity what happened and why."*

Rebecca finds her path exciting but hard to explain to other people. *"You learn to be quiet and wait until you're asked. When people ask me a question, I tell them a little bit. Then I watch to see how they respond. Depending on their response, I either shut up or say a little bit more. When they start getting a funny look on their face, I stop right there."*

She says her path is no place to be unless you're open to changing your beliefs. *"I've changed so many of my beliefs; it's incredible. I think I've been helped in that because all of my life I wanted to know more. I've never felt that I knew everything about anything. I think that's a gift. I've gone from learning about the earth to the universe. Now we're learning about other galaxies. Narrowing myself down to just one thing is inconceivable."*

Life Goals

Each of her group has a different part of the plan. Rebecca said she is in charge of the garden because of her close communication and connection with nature. *"My part will be channeling energies to help create new forms of plants. After the transition, there will be new plants on the earth coming from other dimensions. They will bring new colors and new medicines. I've been told I will eventually combine herbs and minerals and elements into new forms of healing."* The garden is two years behind schedule because of lack of finances. So the short-term goal for Rebecca and the group is to find funding.

Spiritual Beliefs

"God is the intelligent energy of love; he is all love energy. We are part of that God, all that is."

Rebecca believes the earth is preparing to go into another dimension, and that she is part of a team working to prepare humanity and the earth for that. Her group and others are being taught the Ascension process by their guides. To prepare for it, they have been told by their guidance to go on special diets, do rebirthing, and detoxify their bodies. She says they are learning it one step at a time and will eventually teach it to others.

Rebecca believes in dark forces because of her own experiences with them. *"Everything I know and teach has been learned through experience, unfortunately."* She said the dark forces were a part of God or love energy who used their free will to go away from God. *"It's a final battle between the dark and the light that's going on everywhere. The dark forces feed off our negative energy. To make ourselves less vulnerable to them, we have to rid ourselves of negative energy, thoughts, and feelings."* Rebecca believes knowing how to protect oneself against the dark forces is important for spiritual travelers.

Her group's guides have told them that the separation of light and dark is coming. *"The dark forces and human beings who choose to live in fear, anger, and hatred will be removed from the earth. The loving ones who work with God have been subject to this negative energy too long, and it's time to end it."*

Intuition, Reason, and Emotion

Part of her growth process is learning to master all of her bodies, including the emotional body. *"Mastery doesn't imply being a special person. Mastery implies being a master of who you are. It's what we are all here to work on"*

Rebecca said that emotions are different from feelings. *"Emotions come and go with highs and lows. A feeling is more like an intuition. Something feels right and you just feel you know what to do. You feel a part of God."*

She used intuition to buy the property and the newspaper. But she used her reason and logic to build her house and to run the newspaper.

"The idea is to combine the right and left sides of the brain. Neither one is complete without the other. Your personality talks to you through your reason and intellect and your soul communicates through your feeling, intuition, and heart. What we are here for is to become souls, not egos walking around in bodies. The hard part is having the ego work with the soul, not in opposition to it."

Growth Techniques

Courses in sound, color, and vibration contributed a large part to Rebecca's growth. She uses techniques from those courses to surround herself with supportive energy, to open her chakras, and to tune into her spiritual self.

She doesn't take a separate time to meditate because she is in touch with her guidance all the time. When she asks a question, she gets an answer immediately.

Update (January 1990)

Rebecca finished one of the major projects with her group and felt prodded to get back to work on the garden. When she committed to that, things started to fall into place. She stopped working on the newspaper and at the bookstore. And she has turned the basement of her house into a greenhouse, has plans for a three-acre plot nearby, and has found people who are eager to help. She hopes to get a grant or funding so that she can work on the garden full-time.

She said she has also committed to leading a more balanced life by scheduling some fun and relaxation into her life since she came close to burning herself out.

David (50, Catholic background, postal worker)

David experienced two amazing visions at age eight which he kept to himself. He never felt as if he belonged on the earth. He has used spiritual teaching, meditation, and psychic readings to guide him on his path home to God.

Life Story

David's parents were Catholic and raised him in the church, which he attended every Sunday through his teens. David said he grew up favoring logic and skepticism in his approach to life, and he rarely indulged in fantasies.

At age eight, however, David had two startling visions. One day David was looking up at a blue sky dotted with clouds when the scene began to go out of focus along the edges of his vision. *"In the center, a cloud took the form of a golden chalice. Above it was a white host with a cross in the center of it. I was amazed. I just stood there and looked at it. After it disappeared, I shook my head and didn't say anything to anybody. Right after that my father started talking to me about becoming a priest."*

A few months later, David saw a vision of the Virgin Mary in his room surrounded by a bluish white light. *"I wasn't frightened by it. As the image faded, I felt a warm sense of love I've never felt since."* Again, he kept his vision to himself. And he described the remainder of his teen years as normal.

David never had any particular career goals. His father wanted him to become a priest, but David told him he wasn't interested in that or in getting married. He went into the service and took a job with the post office when he got out.

A co-worker took David home to meet his family one day, and the man's eight year old daughter felt an immediate connection to David, who was thirty at the time. When David transferred to another city, he kept in touch with her.

Years later during a college break, the girl visited David. They went for a drive and stopped at a point overlooking a gorge. *"We stood at the edge, holding hands, watching a hawk. Suddenly, a chill went up my spine, and I turned to look at her. We both said at the same time, 'We were Indians before.' We just laughed it off at the time, but whenever I talk about it, I still get chills up my spine."* They saw each other on and off for a few years and then went their separate ways. But David said he has never felt as close to anyone else.

About the time he first met the girl, he started noticing his ability to feel other people's emotions. *"I can pick up on how people feel about me. If they're angry with me, I know it even if they're smiling in my face. I could pick up on my girlfriend when she was crying at home."* He said that even though he can sense other people's emotions, he doesn't feel his own. *"I think that's one reason I haven't married. I'm not emotionally mature enough for that."*

David is interested in cycles, whether they are related to biorhythms, reincarnation, or the stock market. He started studying reincarnation after his experience at the gorge with his friend.

Since David was twelve, he has felt that he doesn't belong on the earth. *"I didn't know why. When I was about 16, I thought that I would die and go home. A couple of times a year, I get the feeling that I don't belong here. When I turned thirty-five, I told my mother about it. She said she had experienced the same thing and she finally made up her mind in her mid-thirties to stay until it was time to go."*

Soon after, David felt drawn to Transcendental Meditation. He always felt he had to go to God himself without someone else acting as an intermediary. Meditation seemed like a reasonable approach to him for contacting his higher self for guidance.

In 1979, he responded to a Rosicrucian advertisement and liked their teachings which he said are similar to what he has read of Eastern religions. The Rosicrucian teachings, however, are based on the mystery schools of early Egypt, and they include breathing and meditation exercises.

David has past-life readings done every six months. He never tells the psychic about himself, but he gets insights into his present life when he hears about life-styles or illnesses he experienced in past lives. The information helps him understand his likes and dislikes. She also told him about the source of a respiratory condition he has.

The psychic told him that he goes through cycles of growth and then plateaus where he practices what he has learned. She told him the next period of growth will involve developing telepathic and healing abilities. *"After meditation, I can feel energy move through my body when I take a deep breath. I can especially feel it in the ends of my fingers."*

Prayer is also an important part of David's life. He has a list of people for whom he prays. *"The effect on people is interesting even when they don't know you're praying for them. I knew a woman with throat cancer who worked in a restaurant. When I was meditating one evening, I decided to visualize sending her healing energy. I felt the energy begin circling in my solar plexus, and I felt it go out. A few days later at the restaurant, the woman treated me like a king. People were looking at me like I was weird. People respond even if it's from a subconscious level."*

David has talked to his father about some of what he is doing. *"My father's beginning to accept that organized religion is not the only channel to spiritual development, and he meditates himself."*

Life Goals

David would like to have more time to read and do spiritual exercises. He is hoping to change his work assignment to allow that.

Spiritual Beliefs

David believes that God created souls to share in the power of creation and that the soul's ultimate goal is to move towards God and become one with Him in the process of creating.

David said people are here to learn from each relationship. Hopefully, they will learn to love others and develop the desire to be of service to others. *"I try to live in harmony with the divine will. I pray for my boss to be more understanding and tolerant of me. But I don't get upset if that doesn't happen. It may be necessary for my growth."*

Humans create the conditions of evil around them. Karma is the consequence of each action as it returns to the originator of the action. David said the human aura can be strengthened through certain exercises to prevent external negative influences.

Growth Techniques

David has benefitted from meditation, prayer, psychic readings, and the Rosicrucian teachings. *"If you want something that is more important than what the material world has to offer, you should persevere in going for it. The difference between a saint and a sinner is that the sinner gave up."*

Terri (35, Methodist background, governess)

Terri's first out-of-body experience came when she was four. Her father died when she was six, her brother died when she was eight, and she was separated from her mother a year later. Drawing from a background of trauma and emotional abuse, she now goes from family to family as a governess raising troubled children and healing her own wounds.

Life Story

Terri's emotional conflicts started as early as age three when her Pentecostal grandmother told Terri she would go to hell if she ever cut her hair. Before entering first grade, her other grandmother wanted to trim her hair. Remembering the dire consequences, Terri had to be tied into a chair before her grandmother could cut her hair. *"I hate to see what churches do to children's minds. I think you should unfold them, not mold them. I think religion did me a lot of harm. All the talk about bad people, the devil, and hell scared the — — out of me."* Every night in bed, Terri thought she was going to die, and she thought about what she did that day that would send her to hell.

At four, Terri had her first out-of-body experience. She slept in the living room with her sister on a sleeper sofa and could see a red dot on the oven through the doorway. When she couldn't go to sleep, she stared at that red dot. *"One night, I saw the dot turn into a barrel that tumbled toward me. Then I left my body. I saw my parents in their room, checked on my little brother, and saw my body. I knew it had something to do with spirituality and that it would separate me from other people some day."* Terri didn't tell her parents about leaving her body because of their strict traditional beliefs.

Terri continued to leave her body and said the experience showed her that life didn't end. In fact, she began to see it as an adventure. She said she was the only child who wasn't crying on the first day of school. Her independence and courage grew and were to be tested many times.

First, Terri's uncle died in a plane crash about the time she started leaving her body. Two years later, Terri saw her father lying on the bathroom floor, dead of a heart attack. Her brother died of tonsillectomy complications when she was eight. *"I wanted to know where my father and little brother were, what they were experiencing. Those thoughts went through my mind all the time while lying in the dark at night. I kept asking God what heaven was."*

The next year, Terri's mother married a man who was jealous of Terri and her sister. He tried to keep his wife away from her daughters. For the first year, he moved into an apartment with their mother while Terri and her sister lived an hour away with their grandmother and felt abandoned.

Then Terri's stepfather built an addition onto the house that her father had built. He, his wife, and his son stayed in the addition while Terri and her sister stayed in the rest of the house. Her stepfather and mother worked together, went out to dinner, and came home after Terri and her sister were in bed. *"We had to call for permission to see our mother in our own house. We were allowed to see her every Saturday afternoon when she took us shopping. She tried to compensate for the lack of physical and emotional contact by spending a lot of money on clothes for us. Our friends couldn't keep up with us. But that's when she lost us."*

At age fourteen, Terri read a book from the school library titled *The Dream* by H. A. Hartwick, a mixture of prose and poetry which talked of reincarnation. She often had to stop and think about what it said. She read it three times and asked the librarian if she could buy it because she couldn't find it in the bookstores. *"I had to have that book, so when the librarian said she couldn't sell it, I took the book and left money in an envelope to pay for it."* Reading *The Case of Bridey Murphy* hooked her, and she read more books about ghosts. Her beliefs began to unsettle her friends who finally asked her not to talk about her experiences around them.

Terri tried life as a hippie for a while and tried to convert people to her beliefs. Then she tried college, where she picked up her first Seth[2] book. She said that Seth's writings have served almost as a mentor for her.

Terri quit college and worked in retail sales until the twelve-hour days wore her out. She accepted an offer to work as a governess in Colorado and pursued her New Age interests there. After a few years, she moved to Florida to work with another family whose children needed help.

One of her charges had kept secret that a man had sexually molested her in a store. She revealed the secret four years later when Terri came. The girl's father didn't understand why his daughter had not told him. But Terri knew how communication can shut down between parents and their children.

At the time of the interview, Terri was with a new family where she hoped to get the children to the point where they could continue growing without her. The father is open-minded about her spiritual views. He teaches his children about being Jewish, their mother teaches them about being Christian, and Terri tells them about New Age spiritual beliefs. The father wants the children to make their own choices about careers and religion.

At one time, Terri wanted to marry and have four children, but not now after raising as many children as she already has. For her, this lifetime is for looking inward. She has had good relationships in the past and would welcome one, but she doesn't need one. She enjoys her many friendships with men and women.

In addition to helping to heal the children she works with, Terri concentrates on healing her own childhood wounds. She finally confronted her stepfather with how she felt about the way he treated her and her sister. Clearing the air brought tears to both of them. When Terri left, her stepfather kissed her for the first time. She was glad she had the chance to clear up her feelings about him since he died a few months later.

When she went home to help her mother pack up her stepfather's belongings, Terri took some books and subliminal tapes for her. Her mother had stopped remembering dreams when her first husband died. Later, she called Terri to say she had started remembering dreams. She has asked Terri for more tapes to help with other problems. But her mother firmly states that Jesus Christ is her savior, and Terri accepts that but asks her to keep an open mind for other things that may help.

---

2. Seth is a non-physical entity or energy personality who channeled several metaphysical books through Jane Roberts starting in the late 1960's.

Terri described a recent visit with her mother. *"I started laying into her about my feelings about my childhood. But when I saw my mother's tears out of the corner of my eye, I stopped. I realized how hard it had been for her and the guilt she was carrying around about it. I realized she had lost as much as my sister and I had."*

Terri's mother has asked her to come home for a while to resolve feelings between them. Terri is torn between the children she is helping and the need to heal her own childhood wounds. Healing in the house that her father built seems the perfect place.

After dealing with the fear of death so early in her life, Terri has found herself helping a few friends and relatives as they face death. In the hospital, she massaged her grandfather's energy meridians and tried to direct him to the tunnel and the light when he was near death. Another woman with cancer was brought home to die. When her kidneys stopped working, her family expected her to die that day. Terri dressed the woman in her favorite satin nightgown and turned on her favorite program-Johnny Carson. *"As I saw her go into a coma, I sat her up in bed, put my arms around her and massaged her shoulders and arms, and said it was time to go. I told her to look for her mother and father because she had been very close to them. I told her to see the light in the tunnel and to go towards it. And boom, her spirit left her body."*

Terri's goals are to teach, heal, and to right a lot of karma. She said she has already come a long way and wants to grow as much as she can in this life. She recommends that people follow their instincts rather than their logical mind if they want to do the same.

Spiritual Beliefs

Terri summarized her spiritual beliefs by saying, *"Grow as the flower grows, and the flower grows correctly. Everything is going to happen the way it is supposed to happen."*

Terri uses the term "All that is" instead of God to avoid the separateness implied by God. Everything is a part of All that is, and she hopes to continually perfect her own energy.

She said she needs to heal the child in her to enable her to help others. *"How can you be loved if you don't love yourself? You have to believe in yourself before you can expect others to believe in you. Then you can love unconditionally even if others set conditions on loving you."*

Parenting

Terri's role as a governess prompted the author to ask for her insights into parenting. Her family, at the time of the interview, has three young children and recently divorced parents. The father has custody, but his business takes much of his time. The mother has emotional problems, and the children have emotional problems of their own, which they express in tantrums and fears.

Terri has used several techniques to make the children feel loved, feel good about themselves, and approach life positively. First, she talks to them often and honestly. She remembers how little her mother knew about what she was doing, so she takes time to ask them about their day. In the morning, she asks what they dreamed about and in the afternoon about what went on in school. In the evening, she asks if they have any problems they want to work on before they go to sleep. She talks with them about God and what it's like to be dead. She also spends considerable time chauffeuring them to lessons to make sure they have a wide exposure to life.

Terri has put one boy into therapy because of his tantrums. She wishes that therapy had been more common when she was a child. She said that adults used to think children would grow out of their problems or that they wouldn't remember them. Instead, children need someone to help them through their problems, and sometimes therapy is necessary.

She doesn't have the children meditate because their attention span is too short. She does have them repeat positive affirmations, such as, *"I am good, I am special."* When one of the children said he was "a bad boy," Terri explained that he wasn't bad, but he sometimes behaved badly. Now when he feels on the edge of losing his temper, he goes to Terri for help to prevent it.

Terri has used subliminal tapes with the children, especially to help them sleep. Occasionally, when one of the children is in the state between waking and sleeping, she sits by him and tells him, *"You will calm down, you will stop breaking your toys, you are good, you are special."* One night after doing that, the child came to the breakfast table and said, *"I'm special, aren't I?"*

She buys the children New Age books, such as *My Secret Room*, about creative visualization. It taught the children how to build a special place in their minds. At bedtime, Terri has one of the girls, who is very negative, visualize putting her problems into a helium balloon and setting it free. Terri tells her that when the balloon is out of sight, the problems are gone from her.

Occasionally, when the children return from church with their mother, they repeat negative things they heard in church. Terri tries to get them back into a positive frame of mind by saying, *"The Bible says that God is your Father, right? Would your own father ever do anything bad to you or not forgive you for something you did?"* They say, *"No."* Terri continues, *"Well, if God is the Father of everyone, wouldn't he love and forgive you at least as much as your own father?"* She said that usually puts them back into a positive mood.

In the morning, Terri has the children use acupressure on different body meridians to awaken their energy and stimulate their eyes and hearing so that they get the most out of school.

Finally, Terri said that children need someone to say that what they are dreaming, feeling, and experiencing is all right.

Growth Techniques

Terri meditates for relaxation and for the energy to keep up with the children. Sometimes she meditates to communicate with her Higher Self about what she should be doing or what is blocking her progress. She also uses acupressure to revitalize parts of her body.

She has received acupuncture to treat pollen allergies. After reading *Dancing in the Light* by Shirley MacLaine, she decided to use acupuncture for past-life regression. She had vivid experiences of past lives that are tied closely to her current relationships.

Rebirthing[3] helped her discover suppressed hatred for her father because she loved him so much and he left her so early in her life.

Terri finds subliminal tapes helpful in getting past her analytical mind. She also reads and goes to lectures and New Age conferences to listen to other people's opinions and beliefs and to investigate what might be useful for her.

Medicine Hawk (38, Baptist background, teacher and medicine clan leader)

Medicine Hawk (real clan name) has lived with his spiritual connection since age three when he talked to Apache warrior spirits. Today he spreads Native American teachings through his own medicine clan with over thirty locations across the country. In addition, he has earned a bachelor, masters, and two doctoral degrees in education. He teaches in an elementary school to support his medicine clan work.

Life Experiences

Medicine Hawk's mother nearly died during his birth. She had a vision of Jesus and angels who told her to return to take care of her son.

---

3. Rebirthing is a technique that focuses on the breath to facilitate emotional release and healing. It was developed by Leonard Orr and is used in Sondra Ray's Loving Relationships Training.

Later, she didn't acknowledge that extraordinary experience because it didn't have a place in her fundamentalist Christian beliefs.

At age three in Arizona, Medicine Hawk crawled out of his window to talk to Apache warrior spirits. When his father heard about the experiences, he nailed Medicine Hawk's window shut. But that didn't stop him. *"I tried to get out of the room by leaving my body. When my mother saw me outside my room at night, she thought I was sleepwalking until she discovered my body still in bed."* His parents told him he imagined those experiences and that they were evil. Their attack on his spiritual exploration led to his eventually losing the awareness to talk to spirits and to leave his body.

After his family moved to south Florida when he was eight, Medicine Hawk met a Seminole Indian boy at school. The boy's mother, a medicine woman, trained both boys intensely until they were twelve. She worked with Medicine Hawk on and off for a few more years. The medicine path wasn't considered occult in that area, so his friends didn't criticize his involvement.

He did, however, have to hide his non-traditional spiritual search from his parents. He went to church during most of his childhood, particularly the Baptist church. He went to Bible school and read prayers aloud in church. He even ran a Bible school at one point. But he wrestled with his church's wish for its members' lives to revolve around it. *"Whenever someone told me what to do, I wanted to do the opposite. But I went along with it to keep my parents off my back so I could do what I really wanted."* He kept his metaphysical books in his car out of his parents' view and often drove to Miami's Bohemian area to read Tarot cards for people.

After high school, Medicine Hawk went to Vietnam. He prefers not to talk about those years, but he did say that he suffered a traumatic event in a hospital in 1972. *"That's when the spirit that now inhabits my body 'walked-in.'"* He described himself and his mate as walk-ins, souls who replace spirits who don't want to stay in their physical bodies any longer. *"The original spirits abuse drugs or liquor, don't take care of their bodies, or commit suicide. Sometimes another spirit will agree to take over the body. The new spirit retains a lot of the former occupant's memories and habits."*

With his new, stronger spirit, Medicine Hawk went on to complete his bachelor, masters, and two doctoral degrees in education. His teaching income allowed him to start his medicine clan work. He developed a set of teachings from several Native American sources. Over the years, he has established more than thirty clan groups across the country. Each follows the same rituals and ceremonies. His clan work includes four publications and workshops on weekends. He fills his evenings with clan correspondence and teaching many people by mail, including Indians in prison.

His work has not gone smoothly. He has received threats and even an attempt on his life from full-blooded Indians who do not approve of his teaching whites and women. (Medicine Hawk is three-eighths Indian.) *"Anyone who is doing work in the light, that is, promoting personal growth and awareness, is going to run up against obstacles. Anything that is freedom and responsibility oriented is going to run into a lot of resistance."*

Hawk said that two other types of people might feel threatened by him-those teaching native American paths for the money and those who want disciples dependent upon them. Hawk plans to spread teachings that can help people take responsibility for their own lives without concern for making a profit in the process.

He said his teachings are for people who are sincerely committed to putting time and energy into their personal and spiritual growth. He puts more than his share of time and energy into his work and wishes he had more available. He admits to being out of balance, however, when it comes to recreation and free time for himself.

Spiritual Beliefs

Medicine Hawk talked of an infinite world of spirit with many dimensions. He communicates with spirits from the plant, animal, and mineral kingdoms. He is lucky enough to have a rat spirit to call upon to find lost items. *"But you have to use discretion in communicating with spirits. Just as there are Charles Manson types here, there are similar spirits not in the body. Spirits are not your slaves and you are not theirs."*

He asks spirits for guidance or their opinion but he exercises his judgement whether to use the information. He doesn't give his problems over to spirits to handle, but instead retains responsibility for his choices. He said that the relationships between spirits not in a physical body and those that are is a symbiotic one, each helping the other in their evolution.

"The purpose of life," Hawk said, *"is to free others, teach others, and to raise vibrations."* He believes that the earth's axis will undergo a shift within the next several years. *"To lessen the effects, people's vibratory rates need to be raised. That's one reason why there are so many walk-ins."*

Growth Techniques

"I don't like to recommend particular books or workshops to people. Each person has to find his own way. What enlightens one person may have no appeal to someone else."

Karen (36, Catholic background, hypnotherapy student)

As a child, Karen saw visions of the Virgin Mary and had out-of-body experiences. With little support from family or friends, Karen relied on intuitive guidance presented in her dreams to lead her through the changes in her life. The dreams led to a move across country, changing her name, and changing careers.

Life Story

Karen was born the oldest child in a traditional Catholic family. *"I felt I was born into the world with a certain awareness. When I was four, I told my parents that I knew them before, and that I had come back to them. That blew my mother away."*

In grade school, Karen went to church at least six times a week. She enjoyed reading about miracles and saints. *"When I was in early grade school, I remember the Virgin Mary appearing to me above my stuffed toys one morning. She gave me the message to pray for peace and to say more Hail Mary's. I took it very seriously until everyone made fun of me. I had a close relationship with Jesus and Mary when I was growing up and went to church all the time."*

During that time, Karen had out-of-body experiences and visits from dead relatives in her dreams. *"I would see and feel things for which there was no logical reason. My family said I had no way to know those things. So I learned early to deny my experiences or think that they were strange."*

As she grew up, Karen found the Catholic faith too narrow for her. *"The church left me with feelings of guilt and never being good enough that have been hard to deal with. It taught acceptance of others while condemning ourselves. I finally realized I was living a life of more pain than joy, and I wanted to change that."* One by one, Karen says her family changed from being religious to spiritual, resulting in less involvement with the church. Today, none of them is involved.

In ninth grade, Karen wanted to be a cheerleader. *"I wasn't the typical candidate. I had buck teeth, pimples, corrective shoes, and was very shy."* But she saw her goal in her mind and practiced every day. When she didn't make it, she didn't understand why. *"I saw it and knew it and thought something wasn't right. So I said the rosary and practiced every day for a year. Then I made cheerleader as a sophomore. I saw the desire in my mind and translated it into a commitment. It taught me about visualizing and perseverance. That changed my life profoundly because I used all of who I was."*

At age fifteen, Karen stopped following most of her religious rituals so she could feel the freedom to explore who she was. *"I didn't want anybody telling me what I could or couldn't do or having control over my body. I still considered myself very spiritual."*

Karen developed interests in astrology, astral projection and other metaphysical studies. *"I could read someone's Tarot cards and know exactly where they were and what was going on for them. I didn't know how I knew, but I felt it was a gift and shouldn't be abused. It proved to me there was something other than the physical world."*

A few times, Karen found herself at the typewriter hearing words and typing them, producing poetry and other writings. *"I always wondered where that came from. One part of me says it's channeling, but another part says that any great artist or musician has that connection. They transform an idea into form. That's how I see the mystical now, putting ideas into physical form."*

Karen moved away from home after high school and went through a period of using drugs as a tool to explore mystical realms. *"I was close to my parents, and I know they worried about me. I stopped the drugs because I knew it was just a phase, and I was much too responsible to let them control me."*

At twenty-two, Karen was very discouraged with life. She couldn't relate to her friends anymore because they were still using drugs. *"They weren't reading books, going to plays, or doing anything with their lives. All they talked about was how high they got."* Karen was having trouble with her boyfriend and was bored with her job. *"I didn't want to die in the same town I was born in."*

In a dream, Karen was instructed to move to California. She had come to rely on her dreams for instruction and motivation. Before moving, she went to the east coast for two weeks on her own. *"During that time I had visions and dreams that were very powerful. I was given a new name. I saw the person that I was on the other side of a stream, and I said good-bye to her. Through a series of dreams, I felt I had changed. To me, the name change was a very personal, spiritual experience, and I felt baptized for the first time."*

Karen moved to California and felt a sense of high energy for months. She taught astrology, Tarot, and dream analysis classes. She continued to get clear and specific information in her dreams about what she should do with her life. *"Sometimes I don't like the information because it threatens my life-style, especially relationships. But I am trying to match the wholeness of my physical life with my intuitive and psychic life."*

At twenty-four, Karen fell in love with a man and went to Europe with him where they studied food and wine. When they returned home, they bought a restaurant. *"I tried to guide the business according to my spiritual beliefs. It was like Zen and the art of filling coffee cups. I realized that*

I was feeding other people daily, yet a part of me was starving. I knew I needed to get back to the spiritual and psychic interests in my life."

After selling the restaurant, Karen took a day job and started hypnotherapy school at night. Her special interest is past-life regression. *"I want to help people make relationships work and help them in their careers and in improving their health."*

Karen regrets she hasn't attracted more spiritually supportive mates. *"I seem to draw linear, practical men to me. But then the spiritual men I've met don't seem to be able to manifest in the physical world. I don't think that being spiritually rich means one has to be physically poor. I want someone who can channel spirituality into physical well-being."*

Karen credits the hypnotherapy course with finally tying her into a support network. Changing careers has been hard for her because she identifies herself with what she does. *"That's part of what I have done to myself. Because I'm an overachiever, taking a cut in money makes me feel that I'm not pulling my weight in my relationship. It's been hard for me to let my partner make more money than I do and still feel that my life has equal value. I think the strong work ethic of my immigrant grandparents is the source of that belief."*

Karen's father has always been open to other religions. He learned about Eastern religions when he went to India during World War II. He is the only one in the family Karen can talk to about her spiritual search.

Karen's mother, however, doesn't understand her beliefs. *"She gets angry when I talk about past lives. She says, 'What do you mean someone married my husband before.'"* One of Karen's sisters is afraid of her own psychic and intuitive abilities, but her other sister is open to the possibilities.

Life Goals

Karen wants to feel free to take the initiative in her relationship without worrying about her partner's reaction. She would also like to let go of guilt and self-punishment. *"I was trained by the eyebrow. When my mother raised her eyebrow, I knew I was in for it. So I am very conscious of people's reactions, and I usually overreact to them."*

Karen wants to develop her talents working with color and sound. *"I know how colors affect me. I know that energy blocks can be broken up with sound, and I know that working with them will be part of my path."*

Spiritual Beliefs

Karen feels that a person's relationship to pain is an important factor in whether they consciously pursue a spiritual path. *"If people try to avoid pain, they turn to drugs, alcohol, sleep, and television. None of those are bad on their own; it's the motive behind their use. If you deny the pain, you can create illness. If you deal with it, you can move forward, becoming a happier, fuller being. Even though I dislike the pain, there is a sweetness because I know the blocks become doorways.*"

Karen's beliefs help her understand why certain people cross her path and why she has difficulties at certain times. "*I know that everyone teaches me something. It's not coincidental that they're in my life. I know that we're reflections of each other. What I dislike in someone else often points to what I dislike in myself or something I repress.*"

Karen has found that healing past-life situations has brought more positive and easier flowing energy into her life. "*It takes going back into that lifetime to reframe and recreate the situation. Once that's done and your psyche accepts it, then the physical life here changes.*"

Karen believes humans are light beings who have come into physical form to experience and physically create. "*A special interest of mine is how we manifest health, illness, and money. It is manifested through repeated thought. Repeated negative thoughts like anger, self-negation, and frustration often result in illness. We need to learn where our thoughts are. This life is a school and a lesson.*"

To Karen, we are all a part of God, and God is in all of us. "*I have no idea if there is a master mind. I think there are layers and layers of energy. I don't know how high it goes. But I think we are all facets of that and teachers to each other.*"

Intuition, Reason, and Emotion

Karen's mother and sisters are very emotional. Karen feels she favors her father, who is rational and intuitive. "*I've been afraid of my emotions because I thought they would control me. I wanted to feel the positive emotions but not the negative ones. I am discovering the more positive aspects of all my emotions. The hypnotherapy class is helpful because things lodge in the emotions. That is where the power is. I'm letting myself feel the depression, abandonment, and anger that I didn't want to feel before. Those are issues that are important for me to resolve.*"

Growth Techniques

Karen has used Tarot, astrology and self-hypnosis to guide her on her path. "*I tend not to ask the Tarot cards what I should do in a particular situation unless I really want to know because I know they will tell me. Astrology shows an inclination towards certain types of thought and behavior, but we can always change it.*"

Karen uses self-hypnosis and acupuncture to explore her past lives. "*It's like a 3-D movie. I see it and know who each character is even though they don't look like what they do in this life. I've gotten insight into why I feel certain* things. *I use past-life exploration when someone is giving me a lot of grief. Once I discover the cause, something changes inside me, and that person reacts differently to me."*

"A part of me needs to communicate what I discover. So it frustrates me when I find no interest from other players in the drama. But I can only resolve my part of the relationship, and sometimes that's enough."

The Future

Karen is very positive about the future. *"I think we're going to find a solution to the world's problems before we blow ourselves away. Children are being born under strong planetary combinations right now. They are taking on the future obligations of what our society created. I would like to see us teach them the joy of their particular talents."*

Karen emphasizes change beginning on a personal level. *"I can't stand on a soap box and point fingers at everyone. It has to start with me. I need to forgive myself and others. Corporate greed isn't the enemy; it's what we do to each other in our families. If we clean up our personal garbage, the global garbage will go away."*

Karen looks to people who have "their spiritual act together" to be living examples of love and forgiveness who look for solutions to problems. *"They will try to help people who are ready to accept help. The pain of the life we were born into is the gift that gives us the opportunity for spiritual growth. Transcending that pain is the reason we came here. A spiritually aware person can show others the gift in their pain."*

Update (December 1989)

Karen recently moved out on her own after twelve years with her partner. But they are involved in couples and individual therapy to try to resolve their relationship. *"This major change in my life has been painful, exciting, threatening, depressing, and is potentially filled with great reward."*

See Appendix 5 for questions New Agers would like to ask of other New Agers, according to the answers on the survey.

What is unconditional love: It is not, "I can love you if you do what my emotional programming-my addictions-says I want you to do." It is just love. Just, "I love you because you are there. I love you because you are part of the nowness of my life. I love you because although our bodies and minds may be on different trips, on the consciousness level all of us are alike in our humanness. We are one."

- Handbook to Higher Consciousness

8 Review of Personal Stories

Let us review who New Agers are now that you have read the personal stories. I hope now that it will be hard to think of New Agers as two-dimensional characters who dress funny and wear crystals. Instead, they are three-dimensional, flesh and blood men and women with many of the same problems, hopes, and dreams that non-New Agers have.

First, let's look at their childhoods. Some had happy childhoods, but most came from dysfunctional families, as statistics say most of us did. What were the dysfunctions in their families? Some had alcoholic parents. Some were scarred by physical abuse and others emotionally by words of anger and disgust. And some were sexually abused, although many didn't remember it until they committed to healing themselves many years later. Their parents passed on their insecurities and lack of self-esteem to their children, as they had probably received them from their own parents. Wounded parents have created wounded children for countless generations. This background is not unique to New Agers.

But many in this generation are taking a stand against passing it on to future generations. The scope of this commitment is seen in the numerous self-help books and seminars directed at healing the inner child. These people are committed to healing themselves for themselves and so that they can be an example of a whole, loving person to their children, family, and friends. It is not a New Age process. But it has filled a need for many New Agers.

Healing addictions developed in childhood has also led many New Agers to twelve-step programs, such as Alcoholics Anonymous. These programs are used by New Agers and non-New Agers alike because the desire to heal and be whole crosses religious boundaries.

As adults, what are the hopes and dreams of these people? Generally, they want to be happy, at peace, have good relationships, do satisfying work, and have their physical needs met. Most people can probably identify with those goals. But New Agers add the goal of spiritual fulfillment. They have experienced a spiritual awakening, and when it happens, it takes priority in their life. While this also happens among members of traditional religions, New Agers did not find that environment supportive for their growth.

Another difference is that instead of blaming other people or the world for the problems in their life, their spiritual beliefs lead them to accept responsibility for their decisions, the consequences, and their emotional responses to life. No one makes them angry. They learn that some past internal programming results in anger when it is triggered. They feel empowered by the knowledge that their life and their future can come under their control. So they seek techniques that allow them to release old unresolved feelings and programming that don't serve them. As past programming and pain are released, they begin to sense inner peace and joy and realize that no one outside themselves is doing anything to them. They begin to finally feel in control and they notice improvements in relationships. And they can see the programming in other people and aren't so quick to judge or respond to it.

Now that they have committed to self-healing and spiritual growth, they find that the resources they need to continue their journey come into their life at the right time, whether it's books, people, or workshops. Once they have awakened to the light, they sense it reminding them of the home they're searching for and listen for its guidance in taking the next step.

So what can we say about true students of New Age thought based on the personal stories in the previous three chapters? Once more, we ask, who are New Agers?

• People with abusive childhoods, and some with happy ones.
• People catapulted to New Age by crisis, and others gently guided to books, people, or workshops that triggered their conscious spiritual awakening.
• Some who have always known of the spiritual world but found no support for their experiences in traditional religion.
• People who feel that a material world without spirit is not enough.
• People in search of inner balance (body, mind, and spirit) and outer balance (family, friends, work, and play).
• People who know there is more to health than physical health.
• Some who share the process of growth in groups and others who follow a solitary path.
• People who believe reason and intellect are more effective when teamed with the creativity of intuition.

- People who will often put their spiritual path before their job, relationships, and material goods.
- People concerned with cause and effect at the personal, local, and global levels.
- People who value truth, integrity, wholeness, unconditional acceptance, and realization of self and God or Source.
- Some who claim a personal relationship with God and others who feel a part of All that is, the Source, or the infinite universal energy.
- People who respect all spiritual paths and the right of each person to choose his own steps on the path and to learn from his own mistakes. For learning is why they are here. If they aren't learning, they aren't living.
- Some who believe only in the power of light and God and others who believe in the duality of light and dark forces.
- People who have experienced the joy and wisdom of mystical experiences and dedicate their lives to finding a way to return to them, knowing they were a glimpse of home.
- People who don't think of themselves as physical bodies, but as spiritual beings inhabiting the bodies for as long as they are useful.
- People who choose to rise above the traditional beliefs about human nature to strive for higher, spiritual realms. They choose to look beyond physical appearances to discover the truth of creation and existence.
- People who study spiritual truths as revealed in the world's religions, in channeled materials, and as received in personal contemplation or meditation.
- People who ask questions and check against an inner sense of knowing before accepting a belief.
- People who sense a momentous transformation at work in human evolution and consciousness and in the planet as well.

Clearly, New Age is not about appearances, ritual, crystals, or dogma. It is about personal values, attitudes, and processes aimed at integrating a spiritual and physical life. So instead of judging by appearances, try using the test in the Bible for evaluating prophets. Do they bear good or bad fruit? If they are more peaceful, accepting of others, and desire to be of service, they must have eaten of some good fruit and will surely pass it on to others.

For some additional views of New Age as perceived by Jack Clarke, author of *Life after Grief*, please see the following three charts, titled, "Who are New Agers, anyway?" "Why a New Age, anyway?" and "When is the New Age, anyway?" (See Appendix 6 for information on obtaining frameable copies.)

Who are New Agers, anyway?

People who have the courage to take charge of their own lives.

People wise enough to allow others to live their own lives.

People who don't wait for someone else to tell them what is right for themselves.

People that know they must be content with themselves before they can be content with others.

People who treat intuition as a reliable source when making decisions.

People that attain high moral standards from their own personal experiences, not the dictates of others.

People who maintain the body, develop the mind, and nourish the spirit to create a whole and balanced person.

People sailing their own boats with the universal wind at their backs.

People who climb their own peaks with little effort rather than scaling laboriously their own or others' mountains.

People asking for help when they feel, and then decide, they need it.

People who change their behavior to create new ways of acting in and reacting to the world.

People visualizing what they desire, knowing it will come to them in some form at the proper time.

People who see the good in all things, even when they and others don't always achieve the ideals stated here.

People that exercise their own free will to create their own destiny.

People who know that freedom comes from within, regardless of their life circumstances.

People who radiate peaceful serenity in the midst of turmoil.

People guided by a power higher than, yet part of, themselves.

People who recognize that the unknown is a part of God yet to be discovered.

People seeking the perfection of God while forgiving their own and others' imperfections.

Anyone that views existence as a wondrous experience from moment to moment, especially during times of trial and loss.

Anyone who realizes that life brings changes that need not be feared.

Anyone learning life's lessons rather than enduring life's pain.

Anyone who routinely experiences a oneness with all that is.

Anyone that loves without limits or prerequisites.

Anyone who seeks the truth from any source.

©1988	Jack Clarke

Why a New Age, anyway?

Because this millennium is giving way to an unnamed new era.
Because old methods aren't working as well as they have in the past.
Because it is through change from the old to the new that we grow.
Because we have discovered that, in spite of obstacles, we can change.
Because humans are striving again to be free, particularly from our self imposed limitations.
Because through the ages it is mankind's destiny to continue evolving.
Because a better way to treat our planet and those living on it must be found.
Because lack and strife are no longer acceptable ways of living.
Because harmony makes more sense than conflict.
Because the need to be right doesn't have to dominate our lives, as it has over the centuries.
Because fear has too long diminished the love within us.
Because there is an easier way to live and have joy in the present.
Because the season has come to make forgiveness universal.
Because it is a time to learn from the masters, not worship them.
Because we have powers within us that can no longer be suppressed.
Because our intuition knows what is best, and we have begun to listen.
Because we are learning to sense for ourselves those other realities that mystics describe and scientists are beginning to verify.
Because religion, metaphysics and science are blending together.
Because the evidence of our citizenship in the cosmos is mounting.
Because values are shifting away from material goals.
Because self esteem is finally replacing our need for addictions.
Because belief in ourselves leads to a belief in a higher power.
Because our gift of spirituality can no longer be denied.
Because people know more and more that we are on a journey back home to the source, known to many as God.
Because we are entering an era when spirituality has a more personal meaning to each individual.
Because higher consciousness feels so much better.
Because we can now actively participate in our own healing.
Because no matter what an age is called, our dreams will ultimately be fulfilled.
Because it is time to believe in miracles again.
Because we are who we are.

©1989   Jack Clarke

When is the New Age, anyway?

When the light of abundance replaces the shadow of lack.
When the song of the universe sounds within you.
When the wonder of life replaces preoccupation with problems.
When hierarchies recognize that true power rests within each person.
When you are no longer ashamed of who you are.
When self worth replaces the need to please others.
When you really believe you deserve the best.
When adversity becomes your stimulant for growth.
When you lovingly accept yourself as you are now, though you may choose to change some of your attitudes.
When the acceptance of others, exactly as they are, becomes natural.
When it becomes unnecessary to judge or blame anyone.
When self righteousness disappears from your presence.
When the past and the future no longer rule your life.
When there is no such emotion as guilt.
When honesty takes the place of manipulation.
When your feelings serve you rather than haunt you.
When you let go of your need to win.
When hypocrisy no longer suits you.
When it is easy to focus on the good in yourself and in others.
When you know that good can and will replace the darkness of evil.
When your desire to be happy supersedes your need to be right.
When the lure of revenge diminishes to a mere remembrance.
When you decide to seek wisdom from all sources.
When serenity becomes your normal way of living.
When you acknowledge reality, regardless of who or what created it.
When you can treat today as a day in heaven.
When you see the world as a place to learn rather than just to survive.
When the fear of death no longer dominates your being.
When peace replaces aggression in your heart.
When you finally realize that you are a vital part of all that is.
When you learn to accept the help that God always offers.
When loneliness becomes a time to be closer to God.
When you allow the true inner voice to influence your decisions.
When you wake up embracing the new day.
When all life matters to you.
When you choose to begin it.

©1990   Jack Clarke

9   Changes in Personal Satisfaction

This chapter and the next look at statistical results from the nation-wide survey regarding personal satisfaction and growth techniques. This chapter looks at the results of questions that asked participants to compare themselves in a few areas before and after becoming involved in New Age thought. One category included political and social comparisons. The second asked for ratings of happiness or fulfillment in ten aspects of life. Finally, there were four questions related to health and personality.

The first category found that the average political philosophy before becoming involved in New Age was rated as liberal with only a very small conservative shift afterwards. Figure 1 shows the before and after ratings for each political and social item. Interest or involvement in each area increased after involvement in New Age with political involvement showing the least amount of change and charitable donations the greatest.

Figure 1-Political/Social Changes

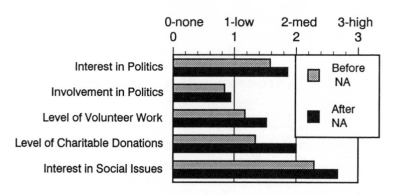

In the personal satisfaction categories, the average rating of the respondents increased in each category with the after New Age ratings. This does not imply that the increases are directly attributable to New Age involvement. After reading the personal stories, readers can decide for themselves what role New Age thought and activities played in each persons growth.

Figures 2a and 2b show the before and after ratings for each category of personal happiness or satisfaction. The smallest increases are related to money (2a) and recreation (2b). While some interviewees recognized their need for more recreation, it was not a major goal for most of those interviewed. Not creating enough money, however, was a common theme in the individual interviews. Learning to trust their ability to manifest money was one of the major obstacles and goals identified.

The greatest increases came in the categories of intuition, creativity, and spiritual awareness (all in 2b). Many of the tools and techniques found in New Age circles focus on recognizing and honing ones intuition. Those who use it regularly find it more reliable and creative than using their intellect alone. While some tools address creativity directly, often it increases in people as a by-product of meditation and trusting intuition.

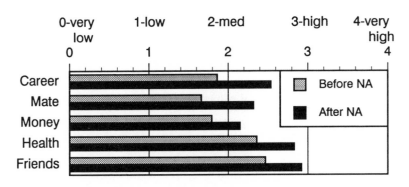

Figure 2a-Changes in Levels of Happiness

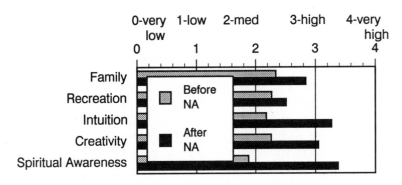

Figure 2b-Changes in Levels of Happiness

The fact that spiritual awareness shows the greatest increase makes sense because finding the missing spiritual aspect of oneself and the universe is the driving force for most people involved with New Age activities. They are searching for wholeness and completeness, which they dont find in looking at the physical universe alone.

Figure 3 shows that smoking, drinking and eating habits significantly improved after New Age involvement. Since New Age considers physical health an integral part of spiritual health, the results are not surprising. And conquering addictions is an important part of spiritual freedom. In addition, many New Age health practitioners point out that alcohol can significantly reduce intuition and access to inner guidance.

Figure 3-Health

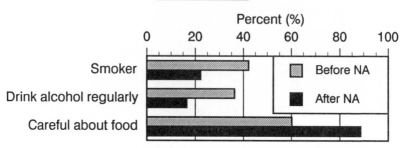

The final question asked respondents to rate themselves as an introvert, extrovert, or in-between. While this is subjective, Figure 4 show a significant movement in self-concept from introversion to extroversion after New Age involvement.

Figure 4-Personality

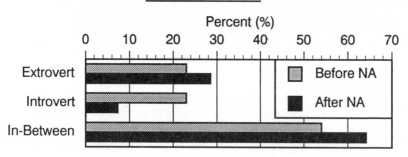

Based on these results, is seems that most people involved in New Age are more social and health conscious, more outgoing, and generally happier with their lives than they were before involvement in New Age.

10   Growth Techniques

The respondents and interviewees have used many techniques in their process of growth and self-healing. But before reviewing the survey results, lets look at the obstacles and fears that were most common among the interviewees. This information will give some insight into the benefits they hope these techniques will provide.

The obstacle most mentioned was old programming made up of negative feelings and thoughts, especially related to self-esteem, worthiness, and doubt. Other programming to be released was being judgmental, trying to control others, and the belief that being spiritual means being poor and suffering. The people interviewed felt these types of programming and beliefs separated them from others and themselves. In order to learn to love themselves and others, they knew they couldnt start by rejecting themselves. So they sought techniques that facilitated releasing old, repressed emotions and provided tools for programming more loving beliefs.

An often mentioned fear was about the inability to trust that their financial needs would be met and that they had the ability to handle money wisely. Because their chief focus is spiritual instead of material gain, they worry about who is looking out for their material needs. They see their big lesson as learning to surrender to the universe and letting it be easy, which Jesus preached in the Sermon on the Mount. Most of the people intellectually believe that the universe or God will fulfill their material needs if they keep true to their spiritual ones. But the challenge is to turn that intellectual belief into pure faith or knowing so that they dont worry about it anymore.

Another obstacle was to see lifes problems as opportunities or lessons and to choose to learn from them and move past them. The goal is to use problems to motivate oneself to do better or to change, not to ignore or try to escape them. When faced with a problem, they know they have choices about how they respond. They can blame the world for their problem, thereby avoiding responsibility for creating or changing it and feeling stripped of power and self-esteem. Or they can ask questions, such as, "What can I learn from this? How can I change? What do I need to let go of? How can I best serve myself and everyone involved?" By asking these questions, they take the stand that they have some control in the situation and that they have choices that will make a difference. Acting as if they have choices empowers them, which strengthens their self-esteem and self-image.

Other obstacles cited were:
- The inability to release attachments and finding those attachments tested. The New Age belief is that the harder you try to hold onto something, the stronger the universe will try to pull it away. Either it will be pulled away, or you will learn that it was never yours and that by letting it go, it is free to be in your life if it is best for you.
- Managing time. Some took on more activities than they could handle, leaving them less time for spiritual work than they would have liked.
- Taking on the feelings of people around them without knowing it, thereby suffering for days or weeks from unknown empathic connections to others. When they became aware of it, they could usually do something to clear the connection.
- Adapting to a world whose assumptions and motivations don't fit them anymore.
- Keeping momentum going day after day.
- The need to feel supported rather than abandoned and rejected.
- Stress on the job.
- Codependency.

Other fears mentioned were:
- Fear of dying before discovering one's mission or purpose.
- Fear of not being good enough, not being accepted.
- Fear of losing security, which prevents making changes.
- Fear of not having the type of relationship one wants.
- Fear of not being able to go deeper or hear the correct guidance.
- Fear that spiritual pursuits will interfere with alcohol/drug recovery.

Now that we have an idea of some of the fears and obstacles that many of the interviewees faced, we will look at what growth techniques were most effective for the survey participants. The growth techniques listed on the survey were: Meditation, Reading, Workshops, Seminars, Psychics/Channeling, Church, Crystals, Support Groups, Counseling, and Past-Life Therapy. Workshops were distinguished from seminars as including personal involvement and exercises rather than just listening to a speaker.

The respondents rated each technique with one of the following levels of impact: none, low, medium, or high. (Note: Those who rated church as having high impact usually qualified their answer by indicating it was a New Age church, such as Unity or Spiritualist.) Figures 1 through 9 show the percent of people who rated each technique as having a high impact on them across all respondents and by several sub-categories (e.g., sex, education, birth order, drug/alcohol influence in childhood, and income) to help readers determine which techniques were most effective for people with backgrounds similar to theirs.

Figure 1 on the next page shows the growth techniques in descending order by percentage rating high impact across all respondents. The total percentages across techniques add up to more than one hundred percent because people usually listed several techniques as having a high impact. More people use reading than any other technique, followed by meditation, workshops, and seminars.

Figure 2 shows the descending order of high impact techniques for women versus men. In general, a higher percentage of women rated each category as having a high impact than did the men which would mean that, as individuals, women have availed themselves of a greater variety of techniques than men. The order of the results are the same for each group except for psychics/channeling, counseling, and support groups. The percentage of women benefitting from counseling was slightly higher than women seeing psychics or channels and significantly higher than those benefitting from support groups. A higher percentage of men, however, benefitted from psychics or channels than did from support groups or counseling.

Figure 1-Percent Rating High Impact Across All Surveys

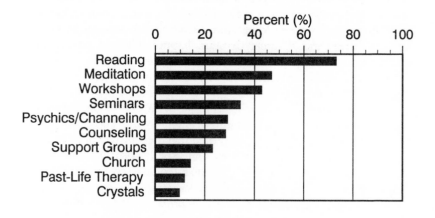

Figure 2-Percent Rating High Impact By Sex

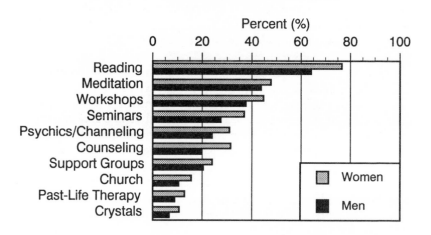

Figures 3a and 3b show the high impact percentages by education broken into four categories-high school or less, associate or bachelor degree, masters degree, and doctorate. The percentages increase with level of education for meditation, workshops, seminars, and counseling. The percentages for reading and support groups increase with education except at the masters level where they take a small dip. The doctorate group shows a significantly higher percentage than the other groups for reading, meditation, workshops, and seminars. This means, as individuals, they have used a greater number of these techniques than those in the other groups. The associate/bachelor group shows the highest percentage use of psychics/channeling, past-life therapy, and crystals. The percentages for church are about the same for all groups.

Figure 3a-Percent Rating High Impact by Education

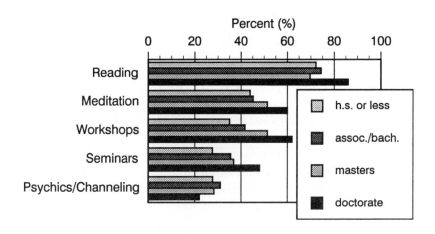

Figure 3b-Percent Rating High Impact by Education

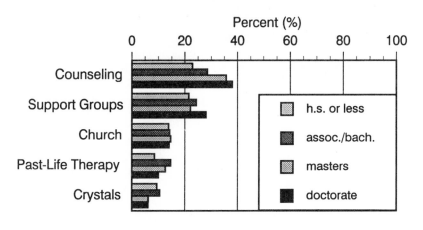

Figure 4 shows the percent of respondents rating the techniques as having high impact according to the influence of alcohol abuse in their childhood environment. The group with little or no influence of alcohol abuse in childhood was slightly more likely than the other group to use Psychics/Channeling, church, and past-life therapy. Since the medium to high influence group had a greater percentage in the other seven categories, it is safe to assume that they use a wider variety of techniques than the other group.

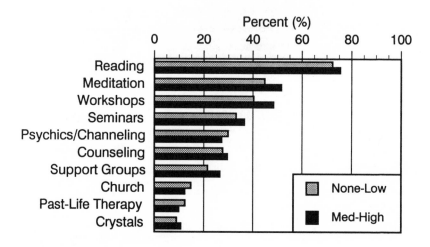

Figure 4-Percent Rating High Impact by Alcohol Influence in Childhood Environment

Figure 5 shows the percent of respondents rating the techniques as having high impact according to the influence of drug abuse in their childhood environment. The group with medium to high drug abuse influence was much more likely than the none to low influence group to use meditation, psychics/channeling, counseling, and support groups.

Figure 5-Percent Rating High Impact by Drug Influence in Childhood Environment

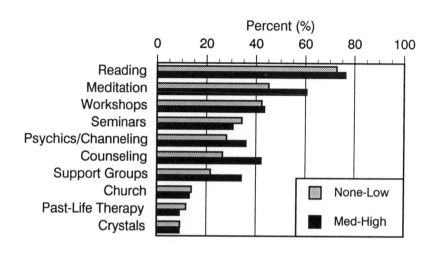

Figures 6a and 6b show the percent of respondents rating the growth techniques as having high impact by order of birth-first, middle, last, or only child.

Figure 6a-Percent Rating High Impact by Order of Birth

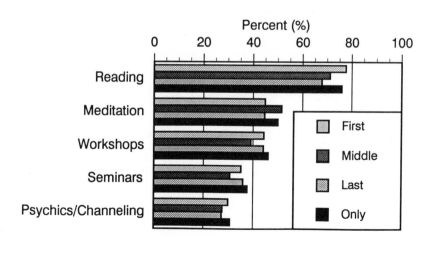

While the results are similar across groups, first and only children are more likely to use reading than the others. Middle and only children are more likely to use meditation, while middle children are least likely to use workshops and seminars. And only children are less likely to use counseling and past-life therapy and more likely to use crystals than the others.

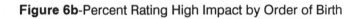

Figure 6b-Percent Rating High Impact by Order of Birth

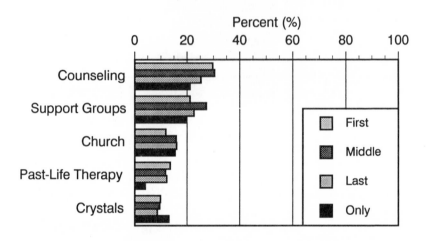

Figures 7a, 7b, and 7c show the percentage of respondents rating the techniques as having high impact according to the type of event that triggered their interest in New Age. The six trigger categories are unhappy with mate, career, health, finances, self, or always spiritually searching. The other trigger category listed on the survey was not included because the range of answers was too broad to apply meaningful percentages.

Figure 7a shows the results of Unhappy with self and Always spiritually aware, the two most often given reasons in the survey. The major differences in Figure 7a are that the Always Spiritually Aware group is more likely to use reading, seminars, psychics/channeling, and church than the Unhappy with Self group.

Figure 7a-Percent Rating High Impact by Trigger Event

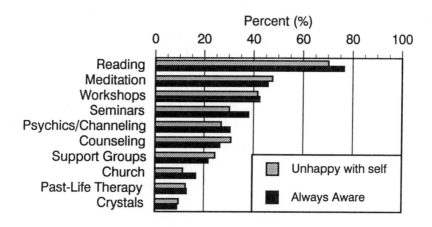

The results in Figure 7b are similar for both groups. The major differences are that the Unhappy with career group has a higher percentage for workshops and seminars while the Unhappy with mate group has a higher percentage for reading.

Figure 7b-Percent Rating High Impact by Trigger Event

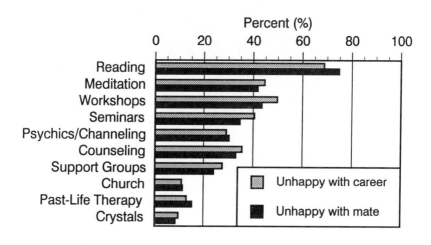

Figure 7c-Percent Rating High Impact by Trigger Event

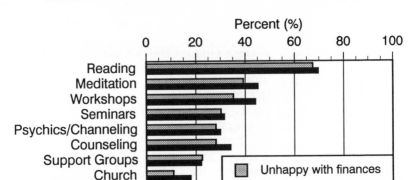

In Figure 7c, the biggest differences appear in meditation, workshops, counseling, and church where the Unhappy with health group has the higher percentages.

Figures 8a and 8b show the percent of respondents rating the techniques as having high impact according to their self-evaluation as an introvert, extrovert, or in-between. The major differences appear first with the introvert group being less likely than the other groups to use workshops, seminars, psychics/channeling, and crystals. The extroverts are much more likely than the other groups to use workshops and seminars, while the in-between group is least likely to use counseling and support groups.

Figure 8a-Percent Rating High Impact by Personality

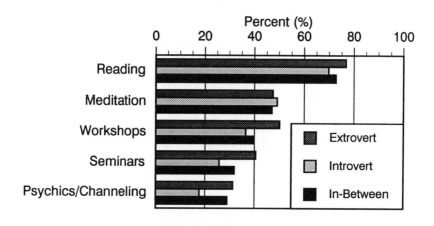

Figure 8b-Percent Rating High Impact by Personality

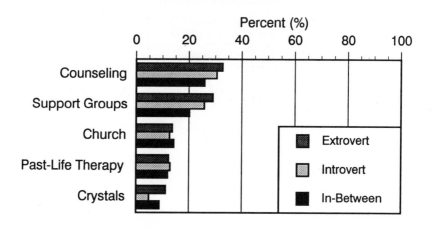

Figures 9a and 9b show the percent of respondents rating the techniques as having high impact by income. Each income group has a range from the top of the group below it to the top of its own group. For example, the group indicated by <$25,001 has a range from $15,001 to $25,000.

The lowest income group was more likely than the other groups to use support groups and least likely to use reading, workshops, seminars, counseling, or church. The second income group, however, was slightly more likely than the others to use church and past-life therapy and least likely to use crystals. The third income group was slightly more likely to use reading, workshops, and counseling and least likely to use psychics/ channeling than the other groups. And the highest income group was more likely than the others to use seminars and psychics/channeling and least likely to use support groups and past-life therapy.

Figure 9a-Percent Rating High Impact by Income Range

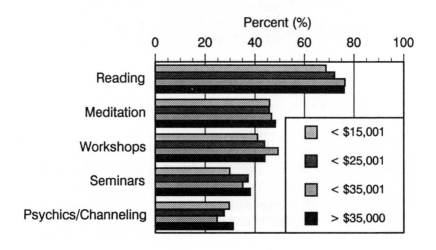

Figure 9b-Percent Rating High Impact by Income Range

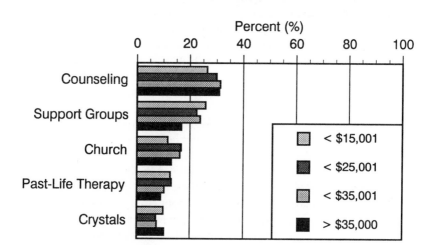

Most of the techniques used by New Agers are aimed at healing and making one more resourceful in dealing with everyday problems. Some people, however, label techniques or groups used by New Agers as New Age and are afraid to have anything to do with them. But many of the growth techniques or groups have been around longer than the term New Age or were developed independently of New Age. These include Alcoholics Anonymous, meditation, visualization, and many forms of psychotherapy.

Some parents are concerned when they hear about these techniques being used in schools because they think their children are being taught New Age thought. Often, they are confusing a technique with a teaching. Techniques can be used independently of the teaching that may have developed them. Yoga is a good example. There are many people receiving the benefits of breathing techniques and exercise postures taught in yoga without knowing or following the related spiritual teachings.

New Agers adopt techniques if they facilitate healing or expand coping skills. And because of that, the technique may be labeled New Age as if it has a spiritual teaching that you must adopt in order to benefit from it. But dont let this misunderstanding deprive you or your child of a healing or self-empowering technique.

Most of the techniques that New Agers avail themselves of could be used by anyone without requiring a change in spiritual beliefs. To use them, you should set goals that will make you more resourceful. You can do that from a New Age, Christian, or other perspective.

Any harm from a technique will come from an unskilled or unethical person employing it, not the technique itself. Always check out the training and experience of the practitioner before trying a technique. The results could be amazing in the hands of a skilled practitioner.

Besides the ten growth techniques listed in the survey, nearly one hundred other techniques were listed on the forms. The following twelve techniques were listed most often by respondents. The number next to each technique indicates how many people listed it on the surveys.

Additional Techniques	No. Responding
Body work, massage	30
Sharing with friends	22
Audio/video tapes	21
Yoga	20
Inner guidance	17
Helping, teaching others	15
Astrology	12
Dream Analysis	12
Buddhist teachings	11
Hypnotherapy, Self-hypnosis	10
Rebirthing	10
Visualization/Guided Imagery	9

For more information about interests in New Age topics, products, or services indicated on the surveys, see Appendices 3 and 4.

11   New Age Concerns

As you have learned by now, the true spirit of New Age is the search for spiritual truth on a personal level through belief, faith, and the personal experience of God or one's Higher Self. New Age thought encourages the study of all religions and spiritual philosophies without naming any one as the "right" one. It also promotes individual responsibility and decision making. The term "New Age," however, has been taken up by some organizations or individuals who don't believe in that sense of spiritual freedom.

In the past few years, the "New Age" market has exploded with books, products, and services. Some people have decided to go after their piece of the pie by creating a product or service, calling it New Age, and selling it to unsuspecting and often vulnerable consumers. This practice concerns people who truly believe in and practice spiritual freedom and integrity. The interviewees were asked about their concerns regarding what they see happening under the name of "New Age." Those concerns and advice follow.

The number one concern is about people who voluntarily give their power away, who look outside themselves for answers. One way people do this is by going to psychics, counselors, teachers, or gurus to ask them to tell them their future or hoping they will make decisions for them. They aren't ready to commit to self-exploration, change, and making their own decisions. They want the answers now. They will invest the time and money in a session to get answers, but they won't take responsibility for their decisions and the results in their lives.

When this type of client goes to a New Age practitioner who believes in spiritual freedom, she may be disappointed that the practitioner won't tell her what to do. The practitioner will give the client insights into her problem, but she won't take responsibility for her client's life decisions. If the client is not willing to take back her power, she will continue to look for a practitioner who will meet her needs by telling her her future. The interviewees considered those types of practitioners to be ones who are either in practice for the money, with no spiritual understanding, or haven't grown enough spiritually to realize they are affecting their client's power of choice to have whatever future they decide. Those types of practitioners frustrate many of the interviewees because they give a distorted view of what New Age is to outsiders or people who have been burned by an ill-prepared or unethical practitioner.

Many of the interviewees advise people who are serious about their spiritual growth to use their discernment when reading a book or listening to a psychic, counselor, or teacher. This is especially true for those new to New Age who are looking for help in a personal crisis and are particularly vulnerable to those who seek power and control. The interviewees suggested the following questions to ask yourself when you evaluate practitioners, teachers, and even books.

- Do they encourage your communication with your inner voice for the answers?
- Do they support your right to explore a variety of belief systems?
- Do they encourage you to test what you read and hear against your own inner knowing so that you keep what nourishes you spiritually and discard the rest?
- Do they encourage you to make your own choices and take responsibility for the consequences?
- Do they make you feel good about yourself and your role in the world?

If so, the interviewees would consider those books and people as examples of the true spirit of New Age and helpful in facilitating personal growth and acceptance of responsibility

The next major concern is about people who say they have the only path to God or have access to divine energy that others don't. These people may take advantage of New Age "clients" or people who are vulnerable in a crisis. They use fear to manipulate people and to develop a following. The interviewees compared this situation to many of their childhood religious experiences. They say that a true New Age teacher discourages a following and that a teacher-student relationship is one of mutual respect in which the teacher values his opportunity to learn from the student. In addition, New Age teachers teach that each person has an equal opportunity for a personal relationship with God which they must develop themselves, with or without the guidance of a teacher.

Unhealed healers is another important concern among those interviewed. They have met some healers who work on others but haven't worked on healing their own emotional, mental, spiritual, or physical wounds. Often they aren't even aware of what they need to heal in themselves. This can be harmful to the client because the practitioner's own lack of awareness about her needs can keep her from seeing needs in her clients that need to be addressed. Or the healer may work only on one or two levels without realizing the interaction among all the levels. Recognizing and working on all levels is the basis of holistic therapies. Those who are looking for healers are advised to find out what the healers have done to clear their own blocks and to heal themselves. The interviewees said to look for healers with humility and integrity.

The interviewees also cautioned people to compare a person's words to their actions. Do they "walk their talk," that is, practice what they preach. It is very important to New Agers to find ways to incorporate their spiritual beliefs into their everyday life. They try to be positive and look for the good in people. They try not to judge. They try to see God in everything around them. They try to remember that it is their choice to feel happy or sad at any moment and that they can control their response to the world around them. They look for people who live their spiritual beliefs in everything they do. People who talk a great game but don't deliver in life won't be listened to for long because the New Ager knows he isn't talking from his heart or his inner voice.

Other concerns from the interviews and New Age publications include:

- "People who use spiritual growth as an excuse to separate from other people or religion."-New Age thought looks toward the sameness and connection among all life.
- "Judging other people's paths or life situations to be indicative of their spiritual awareness. Only God knows what lessons they are here to learn in this life."-A person who appears poor in material things or health may be very rich in spirit with little concern for material acquisition or the physical body.
- "Attachment to results sets people up for disappointment when things don't happen the way they expect."-By tying your happiness to future outcomes, you give external events control over your emotional states. And how can you ever enjoy the present?
- "The media's superficial and narrow approach to reporting New Age."
- "People who are fanatical about anything."

- "People choosing to be victims. They need to know they can choose not to be."
- "Channeled entities. Dead spirits aren't necessarily smart spirits."
- "All the tools advertised if they keep you from looking inside for answers."
- "People who get hung up on one thing and forget to keep moving."
- "People who get addicted to the bliss of altered states as a substitute for alcohol or drugs."
- "The amount of money some people charge for services. I would like to see more sliding scales."

New Agers are no different from anyone else in wanting to be judged on their own merits rather than being judged on the basis of others who may or may not live with the same level of integrity. Actually, they would prefer not to be judged at all, but accepted instead in the spirit of love that Jesus Christ set as an example for all human beings.

12 Responding to New Age Critics

Now that you have read some of the personal stories, I would like to respond to some criticisms of New Age found in the media and books looking at New Age from the outside. I base my responses on the sixty personal interviews I did for this book, the many people I have met in New Age workshops and seminars, and the large stack of New Age books, magazines, and newspapers I have read over the last three and a half years.

New Agers are selfish. Some people who avail themselves of New Age techniques are motivated by thoughts of material gain. In a follow-up letter, Catherine (see Chapter 7) called them "clients" rather than "students" of New Age. A client may go to a reader (Tarot, astrology, runes) for advice on how to achieve some material goal quickly without interest in changing themselves or their beliefs. But students of New Age are motivated by thoughts of personal change and spiritual gain. While many believe that material abundance will be a by-product of spiritual growth, that is not their goal. Instead, they are willing to face their motivations and fears and to take risks by making inner and outer changes. They may change careers or give up relationships in the pursuit of spiritual truth. Their inner drive reminds one of what Jesus Christ expected of his disciples and others he taught. Some may call it selfish or irresponsible, but to the person who feels the calling, there is no choice.

New Age is involved in devil worship or cults. Certainly, there are people who worship the devil, but I have not seen any evidence of it in New Age writings or gatherings.

Most people use the term cult to refer to an organization that tries to control or brainwash its members. Since the spirit of New Age practice is to promote individual freedom and discernment in spiritual search and expression, the term cult does not apply to the vast majority of New Age groups. There may be organizations, however, that have been labeled New Age who fit into the cult category. The rest of New Age can't do anymore about that than traditional religion can about members who present false teachings in their name.

New Agers have no regard for reason. Most New Agers value reason as a tool to evaluate their intuition or inner guidance to see how well it applies to their real-life situation. It was clear from the people interviewed that they sought balance between their reason, intuition, and emotions. They used intuition alone only when they had no time to reason the answer. Intuition is often the source of new ideas or creative solutions to existing problems. Reason is used next to take the steps necessary in the physical world to turn the idea into reality.

New Age beliefs, activities, and experience cannot be scientifically validated. If a scientific yardstick were used against any religion or spiritual teaching, it would fall short. Who can prove scientifically the beliefs, accounts, and promises in any of the major religions? If this criticism is to be used against New Age, it should be applied to all spiritual teachings.

New Age practices entail odd rituals. Yes, many New Agers have established ritual in their spiritual practices. Some use crystals, colored candles, chanting, meditation, pendulums, and home-made altars in front of which they meditate or pray. Of course, traditional religion is not without ritual. It is part of every service, and there are special rituals for specific events in the year. Someone unfamiliar with the Catholic church would probably be amazed at the rituals he would find there. Many people in New Age who came from traditional religious backgrounds have created ritual in their practices because they enjoyed the rituals of their church. The purpose is the same-to keep them aware of their spiritual beliefs and to honor their concept of God.

New Agers dress funny. The majority of New Agers dress like anyone you'd see on the street. They wear work clothes, business suits, and sport clothes. Some New Agers, however, do dress differently. Some remind you of hippies while others have adopted the dress of eastern religions. Again, one can find "odd" dress in many churches. There are different raiments for different roles. Each garment has a meaning or symbol associated with it. And a minister or priest often wears street clothes that identify his spiritual role in life. So do the clothes of some New Agers represent their commitment to their spiritual beliefs and freedom of expression. They are not afraid to be who they are. So you can laugh at their clothes, but they are serious about their beliefs.

If everything is God in New Age, then New Agers do not distinguish between good and evil, and anything goes. To the New Ager, there is more to the "everything is God" concept. If everything is God, then each person is a part of God and each other. Therefore, they reason, "If I steal from my brother, I steal from myself. If I harm my brother, I harm myself." That belief along with the concept of karma, which says you reap what you sow (even across lifetimes), becomes a strong internal voice that keeps them aware of the potential consequences of their actions. Rather than thinking of themselves as God and above law and consequences, they see themselves as a part of God, whose every thought and action has an unseen impact on all the rest of God's creation. Therefore, they think more about the potential consequences of their actions when they make decisions than the average person does. And while they may feel guilty when something they do turns out to hurt someone else, they prefer not to wallow in the guilt. Instead, they try to learn from the mistake and do their best not to repeat it. But they see no benefit in carrying guilt once the lesson has been learned.

This criticism appears to be a projection of a human mind untouched by spiritual truth. It sounds like a mind concerned with material acquisition imagining what it would do if it believed there were no difference between good and evil. But as the human mind contemplates and realizes spiritual truths, its consciousness is changed. This happens regardless of the path one is on, New Age or traditional. The words of the spiritual masters are lifted from the written page and etched on the human heart, transforming personal motivations. One no longer avoids doing "evil" because of fear of outside punishment or seeks to escape the consequences of "evil" acts; instead, one lives from the law of God or oneness that is inside. To one who hasn't experienced this, it may be a difficult concept to imagine.

New Agers don't practice what they preach. How is this measured? I think the writer assumed the only deeds that qualified were organized social, political, or environmental activism. As you learned in some of the interviews, New Agers believe they have to attain some level of inner peace before they go out in the world or they will take conflict or anger into their activity. Bob (from Chapter 6) was a good example of that. After a lot of work in the peace movement, he discovered how much anger he carried around. He knew it was impossible for him to bring peace to others if he hadn't first brought it to himself. How could he know what peace really was. Now that he has let go of that anger, he serves the planet by teaching children and setting an example of an adult who is at peace with himself. He feels he can serve the cause of peace by living peacefully every day, knowing he effects everyone he meets.

Most New Agers actually make the transition from words to deeds every day because their beliefs affect their attitude toward relationships and work. They make decisions and take action after considering the possible outcomes, usually choosing the action that is most respectful to everyone involved.

The attitude of being of service seems to be a common development in most New Agers. In a trying situation, they ask themselves how they can be of service to others involved and still achieve the desired goals.

In determining whether someone practices what they preach, we should allow them the freedom to determine the form that practice takes. Regardless of the form, we can evaluate it against the beliefs.

When someone says one thing and does another, that is when we know their beliefs are intellectual and have not become part of their experience. This is the way we evaluate people all the time, whether we are conscious of it or not. People will often discount or ignore teachings when the teacher or preacher doesn't live those teachings. When a teacher does this, he does a disservice to his students, especially when there is truth in the teachings.

New Age is a retreat into individualism. This criticism was meant to point to self-indulgence with no care for the problems of others. That point has already been addressed in the sections on selfishness and practicing what they preach. Now let's look at why individual pursuits and experience are so important to New Agers.

People come to New Age through some sort of awakening experience, a crisis or mystical experience, or just feel guided to it. Whatever the cause, the major questions of life have suddenly come to the forefront in their lives. They want to know who they are, why they're here, and if God exists. When that happens, the search is on. And the New Age search is characterized by the pursuit of individual experience of spiritual truths, even when done as part of a group.

Some will try their church again. Others who have memories of their needs not being met in their church look for other paths. They read books, talk to people, and go to workshops and lectures looking for answers. They look outward to ideas, concepts, human examples and take that inward to discern as best they can what seems right to them in their heart. Then they explore that teaching some more. As long as it brings them more awareness and realization as to the questions they want answered, they stay with it. When they have assimilated all they can, they may look outward for more truths that they can evaluate with their inner guidance.

There is an ongoing cycle of outward searching and inward evaluation and contemplation resulting in understanding. For some, the cycle of outward looking stops when they have developed a communication with their inner guidance that answers all their questions. Their concept of inner guidance is an inner voice that they say comes from their spiritual source and has access to all truth. Invariably, they find when they listen to their inner voice, their decisions and actions turn out better than when they don't. Guidance in this search for direct experience of spiritual truth is what most of these people wanted from their church, but couldn't find. It was not enough for them to be told to have faith and believe when the beliefs were either not loving or contradictory.

So they were on their own, forced into an individual search. Some are content to continue their search alone while others find comfort from time to time as part of a group of individual searchers. But in the end, each person realizes that his growth will be proportional to his individual commitment, discipline, and acceptance of responsibility. The group cannot realize or experience the truth for him.

New Age is a threat to Christians. This one I find somewhat puzzling. First, New Agers have no specific intention to influence or convert Christians or anyone else. Again, New Age is concerned with each individual's right to explore and choose his own spiritual path and beliefs. Most agree there is no one right path and that each person has to find the one that is right for him. That means that they consider Christianity a valid spiritual path, just as they do the eastern religions. Therefore, the perceived threat has to do with unchristian beliefs found within New Age. There is no argument there; there are beliefs in New Age that conflict with beliefs taught by most traditional Christian churches. However, that is true of Judaism, Hinduism, Buddhism, and Islam.

So why is New Age singled out? I assume because its concepts are becoming so widespread in the United States and may be feared as competition by some clergy. Also, there is the fear that New Age is in some way related to the Antichrist. My question is, what does a Christian, saved and protected by his faith in Jesus Christ as his savior, have to fear? When television evangelists and church clergy attack New Age and caution their congregations to beware of it, their actions seem to acknowledge a power stronger than their faith in God. What does that say about the faith and God they believe in?

I heard some good advice about this during a panel discussion with four clergymen from different denominations on the *700 Club*, a cable television program. The panel was discussing challenges facing the church. One of the topics was keeping up with outside forces, such as New Age. One panel member said there were too many outside organizations and ideas for a minister to keep up with. He suggested that ministers, priests, and pastors teach and live the Word of God as a example for their congregations rather than use their time and energy keeping up with each new competing idea. It sounded like a step towards effective teaching and peace to me.

13 A New Consciousness

For New Agers, their pursuits are producing changes in their states or levels of consciousness. Some picture the levels above them, some see them within themselves, the deepest being the connection to Source or God Itself. Some have what they call higher consciousness experiences-out-of-body experiences, near-death experiences, experiencing immense love, feeling at one with and part of their surroundings, or experiencing the presence of God. Some have just a flash of peace or joy that is beyond the normal experience. Some of these were described by people in this book.

It is not my purpose to prove or disprove these experiences. But I would like to make some observations based on people I have met in New Age, especially those I interviewed. I found that most were deeply committed to discovering spiritual truth and integrating it into their lives. In varying degrees, their material goals took a back seat to their spiritual pursuits. As I talked to them and many since, I have found that much of their conscious awareness is concerned with a God concept, "right" thinking, "right" action, wholeness of body, mind, and spirit, and being of service to others. I have not found this state of consciousness in many people outside New Age. Although I concede it can be found in a deeply committed member of any religion. And it is considered such a rarity in society that when it results in a good deed, it is reported in the news.

Some journalists have called New Agers' ideas about peace naive. What does that say about our society and our understanding of and commitment to Christ's teachings? Jesus Christ is called the Prince of Peace. He lived a life of love, peace, and forgiveness and had no less expectations for those he taught. He told us how to live in order to have peace and abundance. Obviously, the majority of human consciousness to date hasn't been able to put those beliefs into practice. If it had, we wouldn't be muddling around in war and with homeless and hungry people.

I have seen a consciousness in New Agers, however, that believes what Christ and other spiritual masters taught and is making an effort at living those teachings. Some in New Age say consciousness has to be raised or expanded to perceive and experience spiritual truth. While most people in New Age do not live in a continuous state of higher consciousness, that is the goal of many of them.

One obvious change in consciousness in many New Agers is the change from a material to a spiritual focus. The turning of attention from material to spiritual concerns is something most of society can't identify with. It is a state of consciousness that produces outcomes in situations that don't conform to old rules and patterns, such as exchanging material gains or pleasure for inner peace. People in this state of consciousness may be considered crazy or brainwashed if they give most of their money or goods to charity. But there is a belief system behind it that says God is the source of all abundance and by giving you receive. To Christians, these thoughts are not new. But what do we do when we run into this consciousness? If we ridicule or condemn it, what statement do we make about the spiritual values on which this country was founded and which we say we are so proud of today.

Perhaps a time will come when states or levels of consciousness can be objectively measured and evaluated for those who need that kind of evidence. For those who experience them, no scientific study is needed. People in New Age continue to study alone or in groups in the attempt to find the key to their goal of ongoing spiritual communion with God or God consciousness. Some call it Christ consciousness or having the personal knowledge of God as Creator and Father that Jesus Christ demonstrated during his life. They believe Jesus when he told his disciples that everything he could do, they could do and greater.

New Agers believe the consciousness that seeks spiritual truth and a return to God or the Source is in everyone, but is asleep in most of us. People have, however, been awakening to that consciousness for thousands of years. New Age is just a term that has been applied in recent years to a subset of people who have awakened to that consciousness. The term New Age may fade from use or be replaced by another in a few years, but the awakening of spiritual consciousness will go on. And the search for spiritual truth will go on, inside and outside traditional religion.

New Agers believe that everyone is ultimately on the same journey, whether they accept it consciously or not. If so, why waste time and energy judging everyone else's progress as to its correctness. Why not focus instead on personal communication with God, Jesus Christ, the

Source, or whatever name you use. Learn what you need to learn and apply it. Make sure you live truth and have experienced its fruits before you try to share truth with others, or you'll make a poor teacher. Then, if you are guided to bring what you have learned to others, do it in the spirit of love demonstrated by Jesus Christ. And ask yourself what kind of God you will bring to others-an imperfect, vengeful one or an omniscient, omnipresent, omnipotent God who has provided all the assistance His children need for their journey and knows when they'll be ready to avail themselves of it.

As each of us lets go of judgement and the need to attack, peace will appear where it has always been. One day, all who search for God will find Him. And they will no longer be New Agers, Christians, Jews, Hindus, Buddhists, or Muslims. They will know they are brothers and sisters. Why not live as if we know it now?

The author welcomes comments which may be sent to the following address:

Melody Baker
c/o New Thought Publishing
Suite 305-1380
3455 Peachtree Ind. Blvd.
Duluth, GA 30136

To order additional Copies:

1 – Multiply number of copies by $13.45
   ($12.95 plus 50¢ each for shipping).
2 – Georgia residents add 6% to total for sales tax.
3 – Make check or money order for the total payable to:
   New Thought Publishing.
4 – Write "A New Consciousness" on your check or on a
   blank sheet of paper to enclose with it.
5 – Send payment to:

New Thought Publishing
Suite 305-1380
3455 Peachtree Ind. Blvd.
Duluth, GA 30136

Allow 4-6 weeks for delivery.

APPENDIX 1 – Survey Form

Survey of Personal Growth and New Age Participants

PLEASE PRINT ANSWERS

(Fill in the blank or circle the appropriate answer. Feel free to write comments on any question.

1. Birth Date (MM/DD/YY): _____   2. Age: _____   3. Sex (M / F): ____   4. Race: _____

5. Birth city / state: _____ / _____

6. **Circle** the highest education level completed - high school , associate, bachelor's , master's , doctorate

7. College Degrees/Majors completed (e.g., BS/Math): 1-_____   2-_____

    3-_____

8. City / State where most of childhood was spent: _____ / _____

9. City / State where currently living: _____ / _____

10. Number of brothers: _____   **11.** Number of sisters: _____

12. Birth order (example: 2/3 - second of three): _____

13. Childhood religious affiliation: _____   **Circle one** (strong / moderate / weak / none)

	Never			Often
14. As a child, around people who depended on alcohol:	0	1	2	3
15 As a child, around people who depended on drugs (any type):	0	1	2	3

16. Parents' relationship **now** - **Circle one:**   (married , divorced , one or both deceased , other)

17. **(Circle the letter of the description closest to you now.)**

    a. Aware that something is missing in my life, committed to finding it

    b. Recently discovered part of what I am looking for, committed to making it a reality

    c. Actively working on fulfilling one or more of my goals

    d. Fulfillment and happiness in one or two areas of my life (career, mate, health, etc.)

    e. Fulfillment in most areas of my life, happy most of the time

    f. Other - _____

(Please answer questions 18-33 as you would have *before* you became interested in personal growth or New Age concepts.)

18. What was your job/career _____ , the year ____?

19. Were you self employed? (yes / no)

20. What was your relationship status ? **circle one** - none , casual , serious , married , divorced, widowed

21 How many children did you have at that time? _____

22. Did you smoke? (yes / no)   **23.** Did you drink regularly? (yes / no)

24. Were you careful about what foods you ate? (yes / no)

	1-Poor		3-Good		5- Exc.
25. Rate your state of health at that time: **Circle one**	1	2	3	4	5

26. **Circle the one** that bests describes you **then:**   *introvert / extrovert / in-between*

For questions 27 - 32, circle the number on the scale that best describes you *before* you became interested in personal growth or New Age concepts with regards to the item on the left:

		Very			Very
	None	Liberal			Conservative
27. Political philosophy	0	1	2	3	4

	None	Low	Med	High	Very High
28. Interest in politics	0	1	2	3	4
29. Involvement in politics	0	1	2	3	4
30. Interest in social issues	0	1	2	3	4
31. Level of volunteer work	0	1	2	3	4
32. level of charitable donations	0	1	2	3	4

33-(Circle the level of happiness (0 to 4) you felt about each of the following areas of your life *before* you became interested in personal growth or New Age concepts.)

	very low	low	med	high	very high
33-a career	0	1	2	3	4
33-b mate	0	1	2	3	4
33-c money	0	1	2	3	4
33-d health	0	1	2	3	4
33-e friends	0	1	2	3	4
33-f family	0	1	2	3	4
33-g recreation	0	1	2	3	4
33-h intuition	0	1	2	3	4
33-i creativity	0	1	2	3	4
33-j spiritual awareness	0	1	2	3	4

34. At what age did you become seriously interested in your growth and making changes? ____

35. In what city/state did this occur? _____ / _____

36. **Circle the letter(s)** of the situation(s) or condition(s) that first triggered your desire to make changes in your life? a - unhappy with mate, b - unhappy with career, c - unhappy about health, d - unhappy about finances, e - unhappy with self, f - always actively pursued growth, or g - other (fill in) _____

(Please answer questions 37-52 based on your life *today*. There may be little or no change from the sections above for some respondents.)

37. What is your job/career _____ and annual income _____?

38. Are you self-employed? (yes / no)

39. Most current relationship status - **circle one** - none , casual , serious , married , divorced , widowed

40. How many children do you have? _____

41. Do you smoke? (yes / no)   **42.** Do you drink regularly? (yes / no)

43. Are you careful about what foods you eat? (yes / no)

	1-Poor		3-Good		5- Excellent
44. Rate your state of health now: **Circle one**	1	2	3	4	5

45. **Circle the one** that bests describes you **now**:   *introvert / extrovert / in-between*

(For questions 46 - 51, circle the number on the scale that best describes you now with regards to the item on the left.)

	None	Very Liberal			Very Conservative
46. Political philosophy	0	1	2	3	4

	None	Low	Med	High	Very High
47. Interest in politics	0	1	2	3	4
48. Involvement in politics	0	1	2	3	4
49. Interest in social issues	0	1	2	3	4
50. Level of volunteer work	0	1	2	3	4
51. level of charitable donations	0	1	2	3	4

52-(Circle the level of happiness (0 to 4) you feel now in each of the following areas.)

	very low	low	med	high	very high
52-a career	0	1	2	3	4
52-b mate	0	1	2	3	4
52-c money	0	1	2	3	4
52-d health	0	1	2	3	4
52-e friends	0	1	2	3	4
52-f family	0	1	2	3	4
52-g recreation	0	1	2	3	4
52-h intuition	0	1	2	3	4
52-i creativity	0	1	2	3	4
52-j spiritual awareness	0	1	2	3	4

(Circle the level of impact the following growth techniques have had on you?)

	None	Low	Med	High
53-a meditation	0	1	2	3
53-b reading	0	1	2	3
53-c workshops *	0	1	2	3
53-d psychics/channeling	0	1	2	3
53-e seminars *	0	1	2	3

(*** workshops** - personal involvement, **seminars** - listening to others) -   CONTINUED ON BACK

Growth Techniques - continued.

	None	Low	Med	High
53-f church	0	1	2	3
53-g crystal therapy	0	1	2	3
53-h support groups	0	1	2	3
53-i past-life therapy	0	1	2	3
53-j counseling	0	1	2	3
Any others?				
53-k _____	0	1	2	3
53-l_____	0	1	2	3

PLEASE PRINT ANSWERS

54. Define the term New Age as you view it.

_____

_____

35. New Age publications do you read regularly?

_____

_____

INDIVIDUAL INTERVIEWS

56. A few people will be selected for follow-up interviews, can we consider you? **Circle one:**   **YES**   **NO**

      If YES or if you want to be notified of the book's publication, write your name and address below

      Name: _____

      Address: _____

                   _____

      If YES, Evening/Weekend phone: _____ Day Phone: _____

      In general, what days/hours you would be available for a 1 hour interview during the week or weekend?

      _____

57. If you could ask people like yourself across the country any question about their growth, what would you ask?

_____

_____

58. Are there any New Age topics you would like to see more written about?

_____

_____

59. Are there any New Age products or services in which you are particularly interested?

_____

_____

PLEASE ANSWER ANY QUESTIONS YOU LEFT UNTIL THE END.

APPENDIX 2 – Trigger Events
Leading to Change

Question #36 on the survey asked what situation or condition triggered each person to make major changes in his/her life. The survey suggested six options and included an "other" category. This section lists the reasons given by those who selected the "other" option or wanted to clarify one of their other selections.

	Number of Responses[1]
Death/illness of relative/friend	
• Husband's death	(6)
• My mother's illness and death	(4)
• My brother's death	(4)
• Father's death	(3)
• Death of a child	(3)
• Death of my lover	(2)
• Death of a close friend	(2)
• Lost 2 children	
• Death of my two sons, mother, and father	
• Daughter's incurable illness	
• Death of both parents	
• Devastated by death of three family members	
• Death of parent and following "coincidences"	

Unhappy with one or more aspects of life

- Unhappy with parents .... (2)
- Refused to continue being depressed .... (2)
- Unhappy about the state of human beings in
  general - why are we the way we are? .... (2)
- Very unhappy childhood
- Couldn't relate to teachers and peers
- Unhappy with my parents' relationship as a child,
  always remember seeking answers myself
- Unhappy with my children
- Unhappy with everything, especially my family
- My boss and husband suggested I find some form
  of help because I was always unhappy about everything.
- Hunting for some peace and happiness

---

1. One is assumed if no number is given.

- Business transfer that I felt helpless about
- Almost total loss of self-esteem; became reclusive except for work
- Intuitively knew I was dying inside
- Wanted to commit suicide

Looking for meaning, something missing
- Felt that although my life was good, it was not balanced and something was missing   (10)
- Felt spiritually undernourished   (2)
- The need for a belief system
- Intuitive need to learn more about me and the universe
- I always felt modern religion missed the mark. I just wandered onto the path.
- Met someone who had what I was missing

Inner Guidance
- Interest in books and people who "came my way," would read or hear someone and respond with a feeling of "yes"   (2)
- Spiritual calling   (2)
- Desire to be the best human being I could possibly be
- Timing - I was actively working on improvement of emotional, mental, and physical – next step was spiritual!
- Strong desire came about to start reading all I could on metaphysics - I quickly became driven to do this
- Seemed like a natural progression
- Curiosity

Alcohol or drug problem
- Personal or family member   (7)

- ### Books/TV/Films
- Shirley MacLaine's books   (2)
- The movie, *Out on a Limb*
- Always interested in spiritual pursuits, reading Seth's *Nature of Personal Reality* opened the door to freedom.
- The book, *The Dream*, by H. A. Hartwick
- I became interested in New Age literature through books seen on the job. Then my husband died and I began experiencing psychic phenomena.
- Stimulation from books and friends

Ended a Relationship
- Mate left with no warning after 33 years of marriage
- Getting divorced and losing custody of my 6 children
- Breakup of marriage, loss of home and family
- Ended a long term relationship and lost my job

Psychedelic Drug Experiences   (6)

Psychic Experience
- Strong psychic experience at age   (3)
- Astral projecting at age   (10)
- Mystic experience
- Psychic experiences that altered my view of
  reality at that time

Accident/Injury
- Automobile accident   (3)
- Hit by a car, hit head, started hearing voices,
  needed to deal with it, learned to trust voices

Other
- Stimulation from friends or mates   (4)
- Near Death Experience   (3)
- Transcendental Meditation   (2)
- Introduction to yoga triggered changes   (2)
- Spiritual Reader or Psychic   (2)
- Changes in diet   (2)
- Outside financial circumstances caused drastic
  changes in life style
- Became a parent to my parents
- Trauma of Vietnam war
- UFO sightings
- Always had trouble accepting someone else's idea of truth
- Sexual assault on my child
- Dream that caused me to know I had to change my life
- Spontaneous spiritual awakening on several occasions

Appendix 3 – New Age Topics

Question #58 on the survey asked respondents if there were any New Age topics they would like to see more written about. There were over 170 different answers. I have included one page of topics in decreasing order by the number of people giving each answer.

New Age Topics of Interest	No. of People
Regression/Past Life Therapy	35
Meditation	22
Reincarnation	21
Crystals and their use	18
Channeling	17
Spiritual, holistic parenting	15
Dream Analysis, Lucid dreaming	14
Practical tools for applying spiritual principles to everyday living- business, community, relationships	14
Healing alternatives	13
UFO's	11
Astral Projection, NDE, OBE	10
Astrology	10
Personal stories of growth	10
Native American teachings	9
Relationships	9
Intuition	8
Ancient cultures/religions	7
Herbs, herbal vitamins	7
Hypnosis	7
Psychic development	7
ESP	6
Auras	5
Birth without trauma (underwater)	5
Creative visualization	5
Planetary growth/change/healing	5
Connection between physical sciences, psychology, religion and spirituality	5

Appendix 4—New Age Products and Services

Question #59 on the survey allowed the respondents to list any New Age products and services in which they were interested. There were over a hundred different answers. I have only included one page of them here in decreasing order by the number of people giving each answer.

Product/Service of Interest	No. of People
Crystals	57
Self-help, subliminal audio/video tapes	51
Music	31
Books/mags (for kids too)	28
Energy/body work, massage, Reiki	27
Past Life Regression	26
holistic health, healing alternatives	24
Natural foods/nutritious foods	23
channeling	16
hypnotherapy, self-hypnosis	14
meditation	14
Cosmetics/medicines developed without cruelty to animals	11
Rocks, stones, Rune stones	11
Networking	10
Tarot	10
Astrology	8
Homeopathy	7
Psychic readings	7
Low cost workshops, seminars	6
Native American teachings	6
Spiritual centers/retreats	6
Algae/Spirulina	5
Betar	5
Flower essences	5
Herbs	5
Water purification systems	5
Color therapy	4
Gem elixirs	4
Holistic healing	4

Appendix 5 – Questions of New Agers

The survey form allowed respondents to write questions they would like to ask of others involved in New Age thought. The questions are included as written and grouped in categories. The numbers in parenthesis show the number of people who asked the same question although in different words.

Growth techniques

- What books, tapes, people, workshops, or events
  have meant the most to you?
  Had the most effect on you?   (19)
- How to develop personal power and resist
  giving it away?   (2)
- What are the most effective ways you have
  found to work through energy blocks?   (2)
- What method of subconscious mind programming
  (meditation, visualization, etc.) works best for you?
- Is discernment of the many new techniques difficult for you?

Growth affecting you

- Are you coming to love, cherish, and esteem
  yourself and others?   (7)
- What changes have you been willing to make
  in your life?
- Is your involvement in New Age really helping
  you inside and out?
- What indicators do you have that you are
  on the right track in your personal growth?
- What gives you the greatest feeling of
  peace and serenity?
- What change of values did you make since
  you have become more spiritually aware?
- How do your values/goals vary from social norms?
- How has your definition of happiness and
  fulfillment changed?
- Who are you now, where have you come from?
- How do you grow? Is change stressful or
  do you embrace the adventure with joy?

- Are you more peaceful?
- Are you really happy with yourself?
- How do you verify your experiences?
- Have you found and do you rely on the teacher within?
- Are you ready for death?

Integrating beliefs with daily life

- How do you integrate your knowledge, understanding, and awareness into actively pursuing goals and ideals in your personal life and business?   (10)
- Did your growth change your everyday life, e.g. new friends, interests?
- Do you actually live what you learn or just "study" it?

Growth affecting others

- How do you think your growth affects people around you? (5)
- Do people feel threatened by your spiritual beliefs?   (4)
- Do you find it hard to be around people who don't share growing or prefer to stay unhappy?
- How do you contain enthusiasm for what you are learning around family members who are suspicious or threatened by a religion that is not theirs?

Changes in religious or spiritual beliefs

- What is your definition of God? And how has that changed through your life?   (4)
- What is the most significant truth you have discovered since your journey on the path began?   (3)
- For those who have practiced a conventional religion and have now adopted New Age philosophies, how has your perception of your religion changed and what impact has this made in your life?   (2)
- What is your relationship with yourself and with God?   (2)
- What part has traditional religion played in your growth?

- Do you feel deep spiritual growth, feel less
  critical, and able to allow others their truths?

Reasons for pursuing New Age thought

- Initially, what drew you to New Age
  or metaphysics?   (5)
- Is your search for growth to get to happiness,
  God, what? Will you know it when you get there
  or is the search the goal?
- Why? There has to be a reason for people to
  search in a new direction in face of all the negativity.
- Was there a profound experience of awakening?
- Are you an Adult Child of an Alcoholic or an
  Adult Child of a Dysfunctional Family?

Motivation and discipline

- What is the major motivation behind your growth?   (2)
  How do you sustain your motivation and discipline,
  especially if you don't have a group to belong to?   (2)
- Are you willing to do whatever you are asked on
  the inner and never seek recognition on the outer?   (2)

Social, global issues

- In what ways do you feel your personal growth
  has benefitted and contributed to humankind and
  the planet as a whole?
- Are you looking beyond yourself to growth for
  your community and the world?
- How can we best help the planet?

Support in growth

- What ways do you have of regularly getting together
  with friends in groups to support and aid growth?   (3)

Childhood

- What did you really dream of being when you were a child? And what are you doing now?
- As a child, did you feel different from others?

Dealing with obstacles, negativity

- How do you deal with individuals who exude negativity?
- Have you learned to look at mistakes as a positive force?

Life's purpose

- Do you feel that you have a special mission to perform this life?
- Do you know what your life's purpose is?

Appendix 6—New Age Resources

Charts by Jack Clarke included in this book: "What is New Age, anyway?" "Who are New Agers, anyway?" "Why a New Age, anyway?" and "When is the New Age, anyway?" Frameable copies are available in metaphysical bookstores (distributed by New Leaf) or from Personal Pathways Press, 2272 Powers Ferry Dr., Marietta, GA 30067.

For a calendar of local New Age events, look for local New Age directories, newspapers, or resource guides in metaphysical bookstores.

There are thousands of New Age books in metaphysical and the major chain bookstores covering all of the topics discussed in the personal stories. Rather than recommend books on a specific topic, I have listed books below that give a general overview of many of the topics or activities in New Age. You may want to read one of them first to decide what you are most interested in or go directly to a metaphysical bookstore and wander around looking for the right book for you. Don't worry, it will find you.

Check in metaphysical bookstores or your local library for the following and other general interest books:

New Age Almanac by J. Gordon Melton. © 1991. Published by Visible Ink Press. Objective history and comprehensive description of major personalities and activities.

New Age Marketing Opportunities (Volume I and II). © 1990. Published by First Editions, P.O. Box 2578, Sedona, AZ 86336-9928, (602) 282-9574. Two volume set of resources for marketing New Age products and services. Also contains list of New Age magazines, newspapers, newsletters, and catalogs of general and special interest.

The New Age Catalogue by the Editors of Body, Mind and Spirit magazine. © 1988 Published by Doubleday. A catalogue of a wide variety of New Age resources with short articles and descriptions of New Age topics. A good book to discover your interests if it's all new to you.

Choices and Connections '88-'89:Resources for Personal Growth. ©
1987. Published by Human Potential Resources, Inc., P.O. Box
1057, Boulder, CO 80306. Comprehensive catalogue of articles
and resources for personal growth in just about every area you
can think of. Includes resources for community and global level as
well. Another good reference book.

The Whole Again Resource Guide by Tim Ryan and Patricia J. Case.
©1986. Published by SourceNet, P.O. Box 6767, Santa Barbara,
CA 93160, (805) 494-7123. Directory to alternative and New
Age periodicals and resource books.

The Encyclopedia of Alternative Health Care by Kristin Gottschalk
Olsen. © 1989. Published by Pocket Books. Discussion of
holistic health lifestyle and the development and use of many
alternative healing arts, from acupressure to homeopathy to past
life therapy, Reiki, and yoga. From here, pursue books on specific
topics of interest.

Bibliography

New Age Seen From the Outside

Blow, Richard. "Moronic Convergence," *The New Republic* (January 25, 1988), pp. 24-27.

Chandler, Russell. *Understanding the New Age*. Dallas: Word Publishing, 1988.

Collins, Monica. "Not Some Spaced-Out California Concept," *USA Today*, January 16, 1987, p. 1-A.

Cumbey, Constance. *The Hidden Dangers of the Rainbow*. Shreeveport: Huntington House, Inc., 1983.

Friedrich, Otto. "New Age Harmonies," *Time* (December 7, 1987), pp.62-72.

Kever, Jeannie. "New Age Dawns," *San Antonio Light*, January, 8 1989, fiche 3, grids F8-10.

Larson, Bob. *Straight Answers on the New Age*. Nashville: Thomas Nelson Publishers, 1989.

Mayfield, Marjorie. "A Subculture Finds Its Mecca in Virginia Beach," *The Virginian-Pilot*, January 14, 1989, section A, pp. 1, 6.

Melton, J. Gordon. *New Age Almanac*. Detroit: Visible Ink Press, 1991.

Meyers, Jim. "Channels," *USA Today*, January 22, 1987, p.2-D.

Negri, Maxine. "Age-old Problems of the New Age Movement", *The Humanist* (March/April 1988), pp. 23-26.

Ostrom, Carol M. "An Eye-Opening Look at New Age," Seattle Times [WA], January 7, 1989, fiche 3, grids F6-7.

Sverdlik, Alan. "Once Lost, Many Say They Now Have Found Amazing Grace in New Age," *The Atlanta Journal*, November 28, 1988, Section B, pp. 1, 4.

New Age Experienced
From the Inside

_____. *A Course in Miracles*. Tiburon, CA: Foundation for Inner Peace, 1985.

DeRohan, Ceanne. *Right Use of Will*. Santa Fe: Four Winds Publications, 1986.

Ferguson, Marilyn. *The Aquarian Conspiracy*. Los Angeles: J. P. Tarcher, Inc., 1987.

Gawain, Shakti. *Living in the Light*. San Rafael, CA: Whatever Publishing, Inc., 1986.

Harricharan, John. *When You Can Walk on Water, Take the Boat*. Marietta, GA: New World Publishing, 1986.

Hay, Louise L. *You Can Heal Your Life*. Santa Monica, CA: Hay House, Inc., 1987.

Howard, Vernon. *Mystic Path to Cosmic Power*. West Nyack, NY: Parker Publishing Company, Inc., 1967.

Howard, Vernon. *The Power of Your Supermind*. Englewood Cliffs, NJ: Prentice Hall, 1975.

James, Eliott. *Attaining The Mastership*. Atlanta: Dhamma Books, 1988(1989).

James, Eliott. *Living a Balanced Life*. Atlanta: Dhamma Books, 1990.

Kautz, William H. and Branon, Melanie. *Channeling: The Intuitive Connection*. San Francisco: Harper & Row, 1987.

Keyes Jr., Ken. *Handbook to Higher Consciousness*. Coos Bay, OR: Living Love Publications, 1975.

MacLaine, Shirley. *Out on a Limb*. New York: Bantam Books, Inc., 1983.

MacLaine, Shirley. *Dancing in the Light*. New York: Bantam Books, Inc., 1985.

MacLaine, Shirley. *It's All in the Playing*. New York: Bantam Books, Inc., 1987.

McLaughlin, Corinne. "Evaluating Psychic Guidance and Channeling," *Venture Inward* (January/February 1988), pp. 36-39, 53.

Orr, Leonard and Ray, Sondra. *Rebirthing in the New Age*. Berkeley, CA: Celestial Arts, 1983.

Prophet, Elizabeth Clare. *The Great White Brotherhood in the Culture, History and Religion of America*. Livingston, MT: Summit University Press, 1987.

Puryear, Herbert B. *The Edgar Cayce Primer*. New York: Bantam Books, Inc., 1982(1986).

Roberts, Jane. *Seth Speaks*. New York: Bantam Books, Inc., 1972.
The Christ. *New Teachings for an Awakening Humanity*. Santa Clara, CA: S.E.E. Publishing Company, 1986.
Weinberg, Steven Lee (editor). *Ramtha: An Introduction*. Eastsound, WA. 1988.
Yogananda, Paramahansa. *Autobiography of a Yogi.*. Los Angeles: Self-Realization Fellowship, 1946.

Other

Adler, Mortimer J. *Aristotle for Everybody*. New York: Macmillan Publishing, Co. Inc., 1978.
Anthony, Dick; Ecker, Bruce; and Wilbur, Ken (editors). *Spiritual Choices: The Problem of Recognizing Authentic Paths to Inner Transformation*. New York: Paragon House Publishers, 1987.
Feibleman, James. *Understanding Oriental Philosophy: A Popular Account for the Western World*. New York: Horizon Press, 1976.
Olsen, Kristin Gottschalk. *The Encyclopedia of Alternative Health Care*. New York: Pocket Books, 1989.
Pagels, Elaine. *The gnostic Gospels*. New York: Random House, 1979.
Rosten, Leo. *Religions of America*. New York: Simon and Schuster, 1975.
Rowntree, Derek. *Statistics Without Tears*. New York: Charles Scribner's Sons, 1981.
Statistical Reference Index. 1989 edition. Published by Congressional Information Service.
Statistical Abstract of the United States: 1989 National Data Book and Guide to Sources, 109th Edition. U. S. Dept. of Commerce, Bureau of the Census. U. S. Government Printing Office, 1989.
Stewart, Charles J. and Cash Jr., William B. *Interviewing Principles and Practices*. Dubuque, IA: William C. Brown Company, 1982.

INDEX